SENSING

BEAUTY

United Church Press
Cleveland, Ohio

S E N S I N G

BEAUTY

Aesthetics,
the Human Spirit,
and the Church

John Dykstra Eusden and
John H. Westerhoff III

United Church Press, Cleveland, Ohio 44115
© 1998 by John Dykstra Eusden and John H. Westerhoff III

Printed in the United States of America on acid-free paper

03 02 01 00 99 98   5 4 3 2 1

Library of Congress Cataloging-in-Publication Data

Eusden, John Dykstra.
    Sensing beauty : aesthetics, the human spirit, and the church / John Dykstra Eusden, John H. Westerhoff III.
        p.   cm.
    Includes bibliographical references.
    ISBN 0-8298-1242-3 (pbk. : alk. paper)
    1. Aesthetics—Religious aspects—Christianity.   I. Westerhoff, John H.
II. Title
BR115.A8E97   1998
261.5'7—dc21   98-10280
                                                     CIP

to Josie
and Caroline

CONTENTS

PREFACE

Is beauty only "in the eye of the beholder"? Is the meaning of aesthetics so subjective that it cannot be described, let alone defined? Is the subject of aesthetics so confusing that it cannot be discussed, let alone explored?

At the opening of a course on aesthetics and spirituality, one of us asked members of the class for brief responses or examples of their understanding of the word *aesthetics*. One student answered, "Blue shapes on canvas." Another student joined in, "The ocean when it is green and deep." Around the room there were murmurs of assent and also dissent. The responses continued in great number and in great diversity. Everyone had in mind some desirable environment or space, some attractive work of art, a painting, drawing, sculpture, or other graphic or visual image. Further, the discussion pointed out that we are all conditioned by our culture and history and all influenced by our life experiences. That is to say, what is beautiful in a Chinese brush and ink drawing may not be aesthetic to a lover of Italian Renaissance paintings, what is beautiful to a young African American male may not be aesthetic to an older European American woman.

Granted our cultural influences and subjective leanings, we believe that there are general meanings of aesthetics, a word rooted in the Greek conception of "sensitivity to art," within which our particular understandings, personal choices, and cultural biases are rooted. For example, Japanese and Americans appear to sense similar meanings of the beautiful when they experience the space of Ryoan-ji, a Zen rock and stone garden in Kyoto, Japan, and Chartres, a medieval Christian cathedral in France. While these two great religious art forms are vastly different and open to many different appropriations and interpretations, they have much in common which can be explored and discussed.

We the authors—a college professor of religion and environmental studies and a divinity school professor of practical theology, a Congregational (UCC) minister and an Episcopal priest—are concerned with the broad meanings of aesthetics and with the place of the visual arts in the Christian church. We are mindful of contemporary philosophical and religious interpretations of aesthetics, sometimes labeled postmodernist and/or deconstructionist, which question whether there can be any meaning to aesthetics and which speak of absences, gaps, reversals, and disaffections. While we do not intend to debate their contentions, we do intend to offer an alternative. Further, we are concerned with the connections between beauty and truth—what aesthetics has to say about the real and the abiding—and between beauty and goodness—what aesthetics has to say about the virtues and values which are to guide personal and societal life.

Above all, we two friends and colleagues who learned that our first book, *The Spiritual Life: Learning East and West,* proved valuable to the church, now want to explore the connections between visual aesthetics and various aspects of the human spirit. If, among other things, aesthetics is a way of perceiving and therefore a way of knowing—from the Latin *percipere,* to grasp or take hold of mentally, to become aware of or conscious of—we want to explore the implications of our learnings for the faith and life of Christians and the church. We invite our readers to join us in the hope that we will do what the Russian Orthodox theologian Georges Florovsky said professors, ministers, and teachers do best, namely, profess what they believe at the moment in order to stimulate others to think for themselves.

INTRODUCTION

Aesthetics in Religion and Art

My horse clip-clopping
Over a field . . . Oh-ho!
I'm part of the picture!
Basho

Our habits become our habitations. To make our vision
clear means to unwrap the habits of our imaginations
that enfold our minds and hearts and keep out the light
and the world.
Richard R. Niebuhr, *Streams of Grace*

To begin, we contend that the subject of religion, beauty, and the visual arts is significant, relevant, and timely. Nevertheless, books such as this are rare, perhaps because of a modern disinterest in the philosophy of beauty and a historic conflict between religion and art.

RELIGION AND ART IN CONFLICT
In 1980, Samuel Laeuchli, a professor of religious studies at Temple University, published *Religion and Art in Conflict.*[1] In his preface he recalls two experiences. In the first he tells of being a recent immigrant from Switzerland. While visiting a Swiss Protestant pastor near Chicago, he asked if they might visit the city. His host asked why. Laeuchli responded that he had been told it was a beautiful city with a fine art museum. His host with disgust replied, "Beautiful? Art museum? I preach nothing but Christ crucified." And then he continued by explaining that at Christ's second coming God will destroy the godless people of this sinful city along with their homes and their art museum.

Years later Laeuchli had another experience, this time while visiting a French Roman Catholic church which had stained-glass windows created by the artist Fernand Léger. There he overheard a passionate exchange. One person contended that the windows did not belong in a Christian church because Léger was an apostate, an unbeliever, who had no right to create such windows. The other exclaimed that it didn't matter if he was a Christian or not, for he was a superb artist. It ended with the one saying, "I am not willing to give up Christian faith for art," and the other, "I am not willing to get rid of art for dogma."

So it appears that issues concerning the relationship between art and religion are not academic squabbles among scholars about esoteric problems. Such concerns begin in real life and are experienced and argued about by ordinary people. Just consider in our own day the controversies that have surrounded the National Endowment for the Arts on TV talk shows and the debates about what is art and which art should be publicly funded. And nowhere are these arguments more severe and sometimes violent than in the church and other religious communities.

To be sure, religion and art have been related to each other from the beginning of humankind. A periodic separation and then a remarriage between religion and art have been part of our history also. This situation will not be resolved easily. While a great deal of art from ancient Christianity has survived, so has Canon 36 of the Council of Elvira (306 C.E.), "There shall be no pictures in the church lest what is painted on walls might be worshiped and revered." There is the second of the Ten Commandments (Exod. 20:1–17), "You shall not make for yourself an idol," but there is also a rich history of Jewish art.

Nevertheless, there continue to be several kinds of interactions between religion and art. Art exists in Christian churches and in Shinto temples. Artists belong to religious communities and work in the service of such communities and with the imagery of those traditions. Other artists use religious imagery without belonging to any religious community. And religious communities may have their buildings designed or adorned by an artist who does not use the tradition's imagery.

It appears that religion and art are destined to be both in relationship and in conflict. Further, achieving agreement on what is religion and what is art will be difficult, if not impossible. Similarly, there is no agreement on the nature of beauty, truth, and goodness.

Nevertheless, as a consequence of the historical connection between religion and art and the significance of beauty, truth, and goodness for religion, human life, and community, the connection needs to be addressed and reflected upon by all of us—and not left to a scholarly or theological elite.

Art can represent not only a threat to religion, but can also become a political and personal threat because of its ability to express and manifest a reality different than that of an accepted social consciousness. Is it any wonder that conquerors have traditionally mutilated the art of the conquered?

Further, art makes claims similar to those of religion. It too can reveal the presence and absence of beauty, goodness, and truth. Art can become a new religion, a threat to both established religion and society. Correspondingly, established religion and society can become a threat to art. Is it any wonder, then, that in spite of our living in a highly visual culture, Christian theologians and the church have paid scant attention to the visual arts?

Our existence is shaped and reshaped by our experience of what we have seen. A philosopher who regards art as central in charting human understanding, Hans-Georg Gadamer, put the matter as follows: "The power of the art work suddenly takes the person experiencing it out of the context of his life and yet relates back to the whole of his existence."[2]

Christianity is both iconic (affirms and uses images) and anti-iconic (rejects images). What is the relationship between them? The church inherited the dilemma from Judaism and intellectual Hellenistic culture, but more important are its own theological polarities. For example, the church affirmed that God was one, invisible, unchangeable, and eternal. On the other hand, God became human, acted, suffered, and died. God was transcendent mystery and incarnate human. The first has no shape and cannot be envisioned; the second has shape and can be visualized. While the theologians were debating, the artists modeled and remodeled the God who became human. In time the church learned to live with these two dimensions of Christian faith, but controversy has continued to surround the church and art. The intuitive and intellectual ways of thinking and knowing, the discipline of theology and the art of painting and sculpture can become a threat to each other.

3

WAYS OF KNOWING

There are two ways to think and to know. One is intuitive and the other is intellectual. Hermann Hesse's novel *Beneath the Wheel* constitutes an attack on a world that fosters the intellectual to the neglect of the intuitive. The intuitive, affective, contemplative way is characterized by surrender, mystery, imagination, experience, surprise, and passion. It is at home with anti-structure, ambiguity, chaos, and risk. It is a tacit way of knowing that is holistic, sensuous, mystical, and inner-directed, leading to consciousness and revelation.

The intellectual, on the other hand, is a cognitive, active way of knowing and is characterized by prediction, logic, analysis, reflection, control, and disinterest. It is at home with structure, certainty, and the familiar. It is an explicit way of knowing that is particular, linear, argumentative, and other-directed, leading to reason and comprehension.

While this intellectual way of knowing is at home in the world of time and history, and is nurtured by language, mathematics, and the natural sciences, the intuitive way of knowing is at home in the world of timelessness and eternity and is nurtured by dance, drama, music, literature, and the visual arts.

4

Thomas Merton, the monk and spiritual writer, once commented that while today we have a myriad of instruments to explore things we never imagined, we can no longer see directly what is in front of us! Our thinking and talking about God do not aid us necessarily in growing toward a relationship with God. The church once asked, "What has Athens [Greek culture] to do with Jerusalem [Jewish culture]?" Today the more important question is, "What has Zion [religious life] to do with Bohemia [artistic life]?" And our answer is, "Everything." The arts help us to encounter the holy and the sacred. They provide the means that enable us to perceive life's ultimate meanings. They remind us that faith precedes theology, character precedes moral decision making, and consciousness precedes experience—that our knowing of God precedes our conceptualizations about God. Art is our most profound reminder that we humans cannot live by bread alone. Art and the intuitive way of knowing are foundational to the Christian life of faith. Theology and the intellectual way of knowing, while also important, are secondary and dependent upon the first.

Human beings are essentially creatures who have the ability to experience meanings. One of the most fundamental patterns of meaning is the realm of aesthetics which relates to the various arts. The art form we are most concerned about in this book is the visual arts, including painting, drawing, graphic arts, sculpture, and architecture, in which artists shape tangible materials into subjects of aesthetic importance. Regretfully, it appears that the world of art is more aware of the significance and role of religion in human life and history than the church today is of art. It is time for the church to renew its relationship with the visual arts.

No one has done more to encourage this remarriage than the theologian John Dillenberger. In defending the need for a theology of wider sensibilities, he complains that historically our understandings of human nature have tended to ignore the essential visual dimension of our humanity. Today a new era is birthing, and with it we hope there will be a rediscovery and renewal of the central role of the arts in human life and history. This book intends to make a small contribution to this effort by exploring the nature, character, and importance of the aesthetic.

THE CHALLENGE

5

It will not be easy. Too many church people say proudly, "I don't know anything about art" (implying, parenthetically, "and I do not want to learn") "but I know what I like." Too many are bothered by visual images they do not recognize because they do not want to question their own perceptions or be led to new ones. But where else in life would a person use ignorance as a claim for validating one's own individual opinion? There is a discipline in seeing, just as there is in anything we would do well, a discipline that needs to be learned and practiced if we are to make informed judgments.

The visual arts, like all others, can be trivial and, with respect to religious content or style, banal. But they also can offer profound insight. Recall Paul Klee's dictum that the purpose of art is not to reflect the visible but to make visible.

In her book *Christian Letters to a Post-Christian World*, Dorothy Sayers, over twenty-five years ago, wrote that though we have in most every aspect of life a Christian philosophy we have no Christian aesthetic, no Christian philosophy of art. The church, it appears, has never made up its mind about the arts. The church has either demeaned the arts as irreligious and immoral or tried to exploit and cheapen them as a means of teaching religion and morals.

The historian of religion Mircea Eliade, while visiting Florence in 1957, wrote in his journal a comment on the frescoes that decorate the monks' cells. Affirming the theological genius of Fra Angelico, he commented that his paintings said more in one image than could be said in a whole book, revealing his conviction, as a person who has spent his life expressing himself in writing, of the importance of the visual arts for the communication of religious convictions. The primacy of the visual has been denied and depreciated in the Western church since the sixteenth century. For centuries the aural and the verbal have dominated the church's attempts to communicate its faith.

In his book *Why Johnny Can't Tell Right from Wrong*, William Kirkpatrick discusses Nietzsche's book *The Birth of Tragedy*. He points out that Nietzsche understood people were more convinced by aesthetics, beauty, or—putting it more accurately—by what they perceive to be beautiful, than by argument. It appears that imagination rules reason and not the other way around. Imagination also rules societies. Those with the ability to capture the imagination have the power to influence governments. The greatest rulers, Nietzsche contended, were also great artists in that they brought order out of chaos. They may have been unjust leaders, but they gave the people a bold vision. Perhaps one of the most startling and compelling formulations in philosophy is Nietzsche's contention "It is only as an aesthetic phenomenon that existence and the world are eternally justified."[3]

Kirkpatrick then points out the grim side of Nietzsche's contention. Hitler, an aspiring artist, understood and practiced it. Nazism was an artist's endeavor and artists inside Germany aided him. Hitler's deranged attempt to "beautify" the body politic and his success in enlisting enthusiastic support for his endeavor prove Nietzsche's point. People are more strongly motivated by aesthetic arguments than by intellectual ones. Kirkpatrick asserts that if people refuse to acknowledge the importance of art in human life and community, they do so at their peril. Art can either lead us into an illusion or it can lead us back to reality; it can lead us into an escapist world or it can provide us with a vision. One way or another, art is intimately related to the way we think and live our lives.

Today we are surrounded by media images that are clever, seductive, and memorable. But as Rabbi Abraham Heschel once lamented, our vision is impaired by negative habits of seeing and our inability to truly see. We live in a visual culture, but the church has not paid attention to what people visualize and envision.

Frank Gaebelein (1899–1983) was the first headmaster of Stony Brook School in Long Island, New York. For forty years he developed a preparatory school whose educational philosophy integrated Christian faith and the arts with other curricular concerns. He knew that from the dawn of human existence, humans have made art. Long before we learned to domesticate animals, cultivate plants, or invent the wheel, human beings developed and used pictorial art. From the beginning of human life, aesthetic sensibility and the compulsive need to make art have been basic to human nature. Gaebelein often quoted G. K. Chesterton, "Art is the signature of Man." Other creatures may by instinct create beautiful things, such as the honeycombs of bees or the spider's web, but only human beings consciously engage in art. So it was that he defended the visual arts as central to any curriculum of a school that has as its aim to instruct students in religion.

A renewed wedding of religion and art is dramatically witnessed to in the United Church of Christ curriculum resource *Imaging the Word,* an art resource following the church year that supplements an exemplary educational program, *The Inviting Word.* While we face a challenge in reuniting religion and art, a new spirit has emerged.

7

PART OF THE PICTURE

Sesshu, the great Japanese painter, was the youngest novice in a Japanese Zen temple. His abbot was fearful that his love of painting would prevent him from studying *sutras* and entering fully into the discipline of the community. Sesshu himself began to feel guilty. One day he asked his superiors to tie his hands and feet and place him, bound, against a temple pillar. "If I could break this bad habit for just one day," he told them, "I could perhaps free myself of it forever." But it did not turn out that way for the young painter. Tears flowed down his cheeks, inside his *yukata,* to the ground under his feet. The earth became wet and soft; soon he looked down and discovered that his big toe had begun to move. When superiors came at the end of the day to untie him, they thought they saw a dead mouse at his feet. It was, of course, a mouse drawn with his toe in the wet earth. "It cannot be helped," they said as they untied him. "You must go and do what you have to do immediately."[4]

Art captures us—and we become "part of the picture." Looking at a particular window in Chartres or a special rock in the Zen garden Ryoan-ji, we do not concern ourselves with an academic theory about fullness or emptiness or about presence or absence. An art form presents something immediately and wonderfully coherent; it has the possibility of energy and association with the viewer.

In Japanese *haiku,* the real is not connoted or denoted; it is designated. It places something of startlingness before the reader. It is not mimetic; it is usually counterdescriptive. So also it is with aesthetic passages in the Bible, where in the Psalms, Job, and the synoptic Gospels, especially, the particular is placed with abruptness before the general—the morning stars, the still waters, the whirlwind, the lilies of the field, the gates of deep darkness, the birds of the air, the chariots of fire. Aesthetics today urges us to withdraw from our desire to theorize and schematize and to concentrate instead on the energy and appeal of the particulars—and to place ourselves in their midst.

THE WAY OF SEEING AND DOING

The Japanese word *omoshiroi* means "interesting," but also a great deal more. The word refers to something that is both authentic and imaginative. The word is often applied to a person as well as to an idea, a work of art, an activity. The characters comprising the word are *omo* and *shiroi,* meaning "face" and "blank" or "white." A person who is "interesting" has a blank face, meaning that he or she is not defined, is open, receptive, expansive. We should allow the "queen of the faculties," the faculty of the imagination, to make us open to the statement of a work of art. Friedrich von Schiller in his letters on aesthetics used, over and again, the German word *Empfindung.* It means sensation or feeling, but he broadened it to con-

8

vey the development of an intense awareness of the distinctness of a scene or an object, the ability to stop, listen, see, hear.

As we contemplate a work of art, we might well recall Augustine's words at the Eucharist, "Be what you see. Receive who you already are." Imagination is fundamental to spiritual growth, basic to human life, for it is through the imagination that we appreciate beauty and experience what we call the holy or the sacred. The imagination can be, at times, sloppy and even careless; it likes to throw its clothes around the room assuming that reason and discipline will come along later and pick them up. Some of this disorder is to be tolerated as long as it is a response to the energy of the artwork itself. Fantasy is different from imagination; fantasy wraps itself in illusion and often deception. Imagination, despite its lack of coherence, attaches itself to a work of art and tries not to roam too far.

Imagination is constantly being challenged, particularly as we view objects out of the mainstream of classical art. Veneration of antiquity is a dominant trait of the human character, and we know that art from the past is to be honored for any enlightenment. But we are foolish to value only the past. The claims of contemporary art cannot be ignored. The art of today is that which belongs to us; it is our own reflection. In ignoring or condemning it we do the same to ourselves. We should be ready to use our imagination on the new and the baffling.

Imagination involves our response to the revelatory nature of art. Georges Rouault, the twentieth-century French painter of *Christ Crowned with Thorns* (see plate 1), said that his work pointed back to the age of faith. He commented that he did not feel he belonged to modern life—that his real world was back in the age of the cathedrals. And yet he breaks the Gospels into our modern world by painting an expressionistic head of Christ that reflects the darkness of wartime Europe and the stained glass of the Middle Ages. The painting shows the horrors, the agonies, the emptiness of a wartime era—as well as the problems of the postwar years. Rouault did with paint what the prophet Amos did with words. Amos came to the North from the unsophisticated South, looking at the highly developed ritual and religious activity of the court and the sanctuary—and seeing beneath the glittering surface of the religious veneer the flagrant injustice and social inequities upon which religious life was based. He painted a word picture of the situation for the clergy and the royalty to see. The work of both Amos and Rouault was deemed ugly and shocking, yet powerful in its honesty and prophetic nature.

Chinese Taoism is often described as the philosophy or religion of the "Way." A perspective not given to elaboration or theoretical structure, based primarily on an ancient poem, presumably by Lao-tzu, the *Tao Te Ching, The Way and Its Power*, and on the *Chuang-tzu* (both a person and a text), Taoism speaks over and again of the way of balance, tranquillity, and harmony. These qualities are to be found especially in nature with its rhythms, its changes, its harmoniousness. But the Way, or Tao, refers also to functioning and living.

Taoist painting tends to concentrate, as one might guess, on the great beauty of the Chinese landscape. There are waterfalls, mountains and valleys, wispy and dense clouds, open space, suggestions of birds—all made possible through the artful combination of bold and delicate brush strokes. Frequently Taoist paintings will place a person or persons in the scene. These persons are almost always doing something and in motion; they are seldom sitting still in contemplation. Typical titles of Taoist paintings are *Travelers on a Road, Woodcutter Returning Home on a Snowy Evening, Fisherman with Nets* (see plate 2). This motif is found in postmodern architecture which stresses that art belongs in the workplace and that art should be shown where people have worked—in factories and warehouses.

It is a Taoist insight, much in line with contemporary aesthetic theory, that the beauty of particular objects, places, scenes can only be understood when one is "in the midst." There is the further Taoist insistence that a person should be engaged in an activity while attempting to understand surrounding beauty. The liturgy for evensong at Exeter College, Oxford, contains a parallel idea in its petition, "And make thy chosen people joyful"—glad in their doing and their acting. Perhaps it is true that beauty ought to be a verb. A person who enters the aesthetic realm might be walking on a favorite trail, might be sketching a scene, might be wading or swimming, might be writing, might be gardening.

Taoism suggests that such doing and motion create openness and responsiveness. Activity allows us to shake off preconditions, categories, set expectations. Taoism states that this approach provides a creative emptiness and responsiveness. We are able to understand the particular *virtus*, the strength or force, of water, pine trees, bamboo, thunderstorms, winter blizzards when we stand receptive and blank before them.

There is a Taoist tale, "The Taming of the Harp," about a kiri tree, the king of the forest, which long ago reared its head to talk to the stars and extended its roots deep into the earth. It came to pass that a mighty wizard cut down the tree and made it into a magic harp. For a long time the harp was treasured by the emperor of China, but no one could draw a melody from its strings. The harp refused to make the sounds desired by those called upon to play it. At last came Pai Ya, the prince of harpists. With tender hands he caressed the harp and as he did sang of nature and the seasons, of high mountains and flowing waters, of soaring sky and deep earth—and as he did the memories of the tree awoke. Then he softly touched its strings and sang of the love of these things and the harp sang with him. The emperor asked Pai Ya wherein lay his secret. "Sir," he replied, "others have failed because they sang but of themselves. I let the harp choose its theme and knew not whether the music from the harp had been Pai Ya or Pai Ya the harp."

We should always be aware of the possibilities of our acting, moving, responding. When we are in the middle of things, making connections, significances come to us. Heidegger wrote, "We never come to thoughts. They come to us. That is the proper hour of discourse."[5]

WHAT HAPPENS?

The participative way of seeing and doing offers us a special aesthetic experience. We walk through Chartres and the Zen garden Ryoan-ji; we photograph; we make notes and sketches; we move away from our preconceptions and judgments in order to let a work of art come to us. Something happens to us as we see, do, and enter into the world of art. New possibilities of interpretation appear; different conceptions of the self emerge; openness leads to more openness.

In our participative role, we also sense new dimensions to works of art. We sense the multidimensionality of power in art. A work no longer speaks to us with only one meaning. We might think, for example, of a lake being flat and placid. But it has power coming from its depth. Seeing, doing, moving, responding, taking-in lead to a new spontaneity, involving us in what Heidegger calls *das Gering*, the ringing, or the world's ringaround dance. We can become malleable, pliant, light, and easy in our participation in the dance of beauty.

FOR REFLECTION AND DISCUSSION

1. When have you experienced a conflict between religion and art? What in your life history do you think was behind this experience? How did you resolve the conflict, if you did?

2. Can you describe a work of art that is so much a part of you that you have been "pulled in" and have become "part of the picture"?

3. What painting or art form has truly helped you understand your faith?

I

Understanding the <u>Aesthetic</u>

AESTHETICS AND BEAUTY

A boundary is not that at which something stops but, as the Greeks recognize, the boundary is that from which something begins its presencing. . . . Mortals search ever anew . . . to bring dwelling to the fullness of its nature.

Martin Heidegger, Poetry, Language, Thought

The work of art seeking its realization constantly reverts to the point where it is confronted with failure . . . where language ceases to speak but is, where nothing begins, nothing is said, but where language is always reborn and always starts afresh.

Maurice Blanchot, Where Now? Who Now?

GOTHIC CATHEDRAL AND TEMPLE GARDEN

The great medieval cathedral of Chartres, southwest of Paris, can be seen many kilometers away, across the dips and rises of grain fields (see plate 3). At first it appears as a blunt needle on the horizon; then two beckoning towers are seen; then comes a structure supported by the protruding joints of flying buttresses—and finally an enormous interior where the art of stained glass scatters traces of blue and rose everywhere. The statues and carvings found both inside and outside the cathedral catch the eye. There is John the Baptist, a lamb in his arms, gazing upwards—chiseled with such simplicity and delicacy, showing John's innocence and sense of longing.

Who can describe the beauty of this magnificent work of art, a place to which people return again and again? Surely two aspects deserve immediate mention: the sense of space and the sense of light. Upon entering the nave, glancing around and up, a person is immediately struck by soaring space. It is not only the height of the nave, but the vaulting structure, going from piers on one side of the nave to piers on the other, that gives the sense of ongoing height;

the vaulting seems to repeat itself as it crisscrosses, offering the impression that these soaring qualities go on and on. The walls are thin, not made of the heavy building blocks found in Romanesque architecture. The walls are built out, perpendicular to the outline of the nave, not parallel to the nave as in the Romanesque, permitting glass to be placed in between sections to give a feeling of airiness. Viewed from either the inside or the outside, the walls appear to be weightless and parchment thin. The forces of thrust and compression are dealt with by the elaborate system of flying buttresses on the outside. The buttresses appear to fly upwards, above the tribune roof, or lower roof, in order to support the massiveness of the upper structure of the cathedral (see plate 4).

But, perhaps, Chartres' "girdle of light," as it is sometimes described, is even more impressive. In the thirteenth-century glass-makers' art, blues and reds were the dominant tones. These two colors are always shifting, offering ever-changing patterns. The tones change in strength as the day goes by; at dusk the windows seem to "glide loose" from their frames and colors appear to be floating free in space.[1]

The rock and stone garden of Ryoan-ji, a principal Japanese Rinzai Zen temple, lies in the northwest section of Kyoto, the ancient imperial capital (see plate 5). A good time to visit is early in the morning, or just before closing, or in the rain, or in the snow—times when attendance is usually light, although the garden's beauty survives busload upon busload. The garden approach is up a slightly inclined gravel path, with carefully tended trees, bushes, and plants on either side. At a little distance on one side is a pond with lotus pads and ancient trees hanging over its edge. Visitors remove their shoes at the entrance and take a short walk over polished, creaky boards, around a corner, to the garden itself. Suddenly, visitors are looking at a place that speaks of immense calm, consisting of fifteen rocks placed irregularly on raked sand and gravel—not all of them visible from any given place on the viewing veranda. The space and openness immediately appear as important as the rocks. Rectangular in shape, the garden is bound by a mud wall which carries out the motifs of simplicity and spareness. To be sure, there is structure—raked sand, right angles at the borders, lines, carefully laid out edges, and the uniform height of the wall. But there is spontaneity in this structure. The fifteen stones were placed by the maker of the garden in casual asymmetry. How has this spontaneity-within-configuration occurred? The original designer appeared to have been consumed by the space allotted to him, controlled by it: He responded to given possibilities, not imposing his own designs and preconceived notions of order upon the space. It is as if he had been practicing *shodo,* the art of calligraphy, in which brush strokes are made deftly in response to the given space of a scroll or a defined piece of rice paper.

Sitting on Ryoan-ji's weather-beaten boards beside the rocks and stones, an observer sees nothing of the starkness and sterility often portrayed in paintings and photographs of the garden. Lifefulness and motion in light and shadows are everywhere; nothing is static or boring. It is said that the yin quietness of the surface is balanced by the yang activity of the dragon that lives under the gravel! The garden catches and holds the concentration of its viewers. The quest for meaning is relinquished in favor of a direct consciousness of space and openness. Simply being present with the garden brings grace and effortlessness (see plate 6). As at Chartres, there is a power which bids its visitors return again and again.

17

ALIKE BUT "OTHER"

Is it so strange to link together a medieval Christian cathedral and a Zen Buddhist temple garden? It is not only that aesthetic perceptions constantly need to be deepened, but also that, as works of art, these two have many similarities. Both Chartres and Ryoan-ji state that form and space do matter in religious feeling and perception. Clement of Alexandria, seldom concerned with the meaning and importance of aesthetics, said at the end of the second century that a temple is not a building but only a gathering of the faithful. Chartres and Ryoan-ji speak against Clement and assert that the beauty of a special place has much to do with religious perception and the ideas of a religious community.

Both Chartres and Ryoan-ji urge those of us who enter to use the "gift of seeing without explanation." There are many questions about the form and structure of the Gothic cathedral and the Zen garden, but appreciation does not depend on instruction. Concepts of each tradition are at once visible to the common eye. At Chartres, visitors—including Japanese Buddhists—often attest to the feeling of "providential space," or even of grasping the Deuteronomic proclamation that "the eternal God is a dwelling place, from underneath the everlasting arms" (Deut. 33:27). Westerners sitting beside Ryoan-ji catch, without explanation from experts, that they are in the presence of something standing for directness, serenity, simplicity, and calm. Chartres and Ryoan-ji offer their viewers something to see and appreciate immediately. Each speaks about receiving what is there.

Neither Chartres nor Ryoan-ji offers a proselytizing form of beauty. An aura of triumphalism or superiority is absent. Each, in a real sense, is an unsigned work. Chartres is a product of many designers and artisans who worked quickly from 1194 to 1220 to rebuild after a fire; Ryoan-ji, while attributed to So-ami or Tessen Soki in the late fifteenth century, is certainly the work of many. Those who tend the garden have engaged in continuous work on the wall and also on the approaches. Neither Chartres nor Ryoan-ji glorifies particular human creators.

There is, as the Japanese would say, *hibiki-ai*, mutual echoing, between Chartres and Ryoan-ji. Both sacred places present the art of stones, the muted, subtly differing shades of gray and earth-red. The dull patina and the cracks and the rough edges—whether they're found in the cut and placed stonework of Chartres or in the isolated *hama sabi*, stream rocks, or *yama sabi*, mountain rocks, of Ryoan-ji—offer a similar statement and meaning. The sounds of walking through each are similar—reverberations coming from the eaves and boards in Ryoan-ji and from the walls in Chartres. In both art forms there is *yana*, a Sanskrit word meaning a "way of going"— an immediately perceived way of art's ability to point to a perspective. There is a precariousness in the beauty of each. The gray-brown wall, an important part of the aesthetics of the Zen garden, forming an unabrupt background, is thin and weak, constantly being repaired or touched up. As for Chartres, Henry Adams has written about the "peril of the heavy tower, of the restless vault, of the vagrant buttress."[2]

But what about the differences? In its space, its light, and its height, Chartres is thought to be a sum of Christian doctrine. Its architecture, perhaps even more than its collection of specific reli-

18

gious objects, points to the attributes of God and the condition of human existence. Chartres and other cathedrals have often been identified with the description in the Revelation to John: "And I saw the holy city, new Jerusalem, coming down out of heaven from God, prepared as a bride adorned for her husband; and I heard a loud voice from the throne saying, 'See, the home of God is among mortals. God will dwell with them as their God; and they will be God's peoples, and God . . . will be with them'" (Rev. 21:2–3). In Chartres, the spiritual has become the material and the material the spiritual. The cathedral exists in the city of earth, but it reminds the faithful community of the city of heaven. In Chartres, visitors are pulled down the aisle, through the central space, to the altar—there is a beckoning. But there is also a pull upward, to the arches, to the glass and light—to God and the transcendent Christian worldview.

At Ryoan-ji, the eye goes around and out—around, taking in the fifteen rocks, the wall, the emptiness, and out, over the wall sensing connection with what is beyond. There is the feeling that the outside is starting from the inside. Nothing is soaring upwards; nothing is consciously stated; nothing is deeply intended. Ryoan-ji is not a sum of anything. In the Zen temple garden, it is the surface and the "face" that count.

On the one hand, the differences can be appropriated and understood. Chartres and Ryoan-ji, in their different ways, broaden a conception of human life. Cross-cultural study of religion, art, and social structures has helped us to see things anew. Deep down, insights from other traditions, especially those given in art, speak about something very much a part of a common life—something not perceived until confrontation. Clifford Geertz asks, "How is it that other people's creation can be so utterly their own and so deeply a part of us?" He replies, "Anything imaginational grows in our minds, is transformed, socially transformed, from something we merely know to exist or have existed . . . to something which is properly ours, a working force in our own consciousness . . . not a matter . . . of the past recaptured, but of the strange construed . . . having come upon something [rather] than of having remembered it, of an acquisition [rather] than of an inheritance."[3]

When East visits West, or West visits East, we visitors, with our own practices, tradition, and aesthetics, can be deeply moved in the

19

presence of something different because we can partly understand and assimilate it. Jan Van Bragt reported on a visit of Japanese religious *sensei*, teachers, to European Roman Catholic centers, concentrating on Rome. A Zen archery master was told by others that his bows at the beginning and end of *makiwarasharei*, the archery ceremony—performed and demonstrated in a church—had become considerably deeper than the usual forty-five degrees. He could only answer that he had not been aware of it but that, standing before the crucifix, he felt an excess of reverence which "pulled his breast" toward the floor.

On the other hand, the differences are formidable and real—and scarcely need be enumerated. The cathedral is an "other" to the garden, and vice versa. The art and architecture of the cathedral point to a transcendental reality known in the life of faith. The art of the garden points to a plane and urges the viewer to seek its simplicity and calm. Japanese might well say that Chartres is *tariki*, heavenly other power, and the Ryoan-ji is *jiriki*, present self power.

PRESENCE AND ABSENCE

A long-standing classical tradition on aesthetics has given way. Elaborating a theory of the beautiful which goes back to fifth-century B.C.E. Greece, philosopher George Santayana wrote in his memorable and influential *Sense of Beauty* that "beauty is of all things that which least calls for explanation." He defined beauty as "pleasure regarded as the quality of a thing." He was confident that "its value is positive, intrinsic, and objectified."[4] But today a different analysis and a different sensitivity are at work, the view that a work of art no longer exists apart, objectively able to create a universal reality or a kind of symbolic totality. Today the word "anti-aesthetic" is often heard, that which speaks against a privileged aesthetic realm, against a generally accepted value scheme, against confidence about the beautiful. At the very least, the distinction of Jonathan Edwards, America's great eighteenth-century theologian, is accepted, namely, that beyond simple beauty there lies complex beauty which must take into account "proportionality," or the relationship between viewer and object and between the parts of something known as beautiful. Edwards called attention, for example, to the variable flow of air that stirs leaves of different sizes in an eddy.

A mountain brook may have a beauty, but it is constantly changing; no set description or meaning can be given.

The meaning of the beautiful is certainly to be determined by one's culture and by differing individuals in a culture. Not every Japanese Buddhist would understand and appreciate every work of art in Chartres; not every Westerner would be able to appropriate all of the art forms in the temple of Ryoan-ji. Time and the processes of history help to determine the canons of aesthetics. And Nietzsche, in typical fashion, speaks of truth as beauty—or truth known as anything else. The "anything else," as modern critics put it, could be metaphors, signs, relationships—aspects of human interpretation—which have been poetically, rhetorically intensified and embellished.

If there is nothing totally objective about the beautiful, if there is no separate aesthetic superstructure or infrastructure, we are engaged primarily in a task of translation—bringing forth the meaning for ourselves, our culture, our place in time. As James Merrill's poem "Lost in Translation" puts it,

> *Lost, is it buried? One more missing piece?*
> *But nothing's lost. Or else: all is translation*
> *And every bit of us is lost in it.*[5]

Given the insistence that there are no pervading norms, that no experiences exist apart from many variables—and therefore given the need for translation—can anything be said about the nature of aesthetics? What happens when we are in the presence of something we would say is beautiful? What happens at Chartres and Ryoan-ji? Perhaps two things can be said.

First, consider a principle about home, often articulated by Buddhists. When we are in the presence of something beautiful, say many Japanese Zen artists and craftspeople, we feel "received." Beauty is our home and we are born with a love for home. The realm of the aesthetic orients us; it helps to make things clear about ourselves and our world. We meet an affecting presence, with a message easily understood and appropriated. There is a powerful interaction between an art form and ourselves—an attraction and an attendant gestalt, or sense of a field, in which we are comfortable and at ease. When we enter the nave at Chartres, we sense our smallness in the midst of a greatness portrayed by vaults, piers, soaring space, glowing light. It is easy to say in the surroundingness of such magnificent space, "O God, our Sovereign, how majestic is your name in all the earth! . . . What are human beings that you are mindful of them?" (Ps. 8:1, 4). Something fundamental to our faith is present, and we sense a rightness and fullness about this beauty. So it is with Ryoan-ji. In bare feet or slippers, we round the corner of the temple and there is the garden with its expansiveness, serenity, blankness, particularity. We look at its irregularly placed, odd-numbered rocks in the raked sand and sense a calm in its natural imbalance. Japanese speak of Ryoan-ji's *najimi*, familiarity, and its *utsuri*, real-life harmony. The garden speaks to us in terms we already know. We say, "Life is like that—and can be like that," and we feel at home.

More than any other modern thinker, Martin Heidegger has written effectively about presence in aesthetics, embracing, among other concepts, the ideas of orienting and being at home. He speaks also of the mysteriousness, the "lack," and the confounding qualities of art. In *Poetry, Language, Thought,* especially in the essay "Building, Dwelling, Thinking," Heidegger calls attention to "gathering" as a chief aspect of his aesthetic theory. A work of art gathers its partakers into an understandable and acceptable world. Art illumines real-life conditions and even places ethical components before those who look, listen, touch. Just as a bridge connects, so does a painting, a poem, especially an edifice. The German gerund for building is related to cultivating, dwelling, linking, and ultimately to being. *Ich bin* and *du bist,* forms of "to be," are connected with *bauen,* to build. A work of art allows us to orient ourselves and to rejoice in our sense of being founded, of being placed. Art, in its presencing, leads, according to Heidegger, to good thinking and acting. "As soon as we have the thing before our eyes, and in our hearts an ear for the word, thinking prospers." The lifeful insights given in art will not fail, for "the world's darkening never reaches to the light of Being."[6]

This fullness, this orientation are part, not surprisingly, of Eastern literature concerned with visual forms. Chapter 22 of the *I Ching,* or *Book of Changes*—a chapter called *Pi* or Grace, commenting on the beauty of form—shows a hexagram of yin and yang lines, broken in the middle and solid across, respectively. The hexagram pictures fire and a mountain. The commentary states that the meaning of the hexagram is that fire breaks out of the secret depths of the earth; it rises up, displays, and beautifies the mountain. The beauty in the light of the fire shows a way to travel on the mountain and it can lead a person home.

Second—and so different from *najimi,* familiarity, and *bauen,* orienting—aesthetics bursts things open and leaves us homeless. Even in the midst of being received and oriented, we confess that something is not fully present. In the rabbinic narratives of Judaism, there are stories which familiarize the reader, bringing biblical concepts close to home, but there are stories which de-familiarize, producing consternation, questioning, and lack of resolution. When we say, "Oh, it's too beautiful," we are often alluding to more than our loss for words. The foliage of a New England October cannot be taken in; its surrounding glory does not allow us a place to rest the eye; we feel disquieted, even overwhelmed by the reds and the yellows. We stand in the midst of something that eludes us, something that cuts at our calm and composure.

23

Why this uneasiness? Why this "fierce rhetoric," as the Vedic tradition would say? Something is disturbing: We may even have the feeling of wanting to escape. The bare trees of November are more easily accepted by our eyes. In the beauty of a Zen temple, about to begin *zazen,* meditation, we may look for the way out. In the middle of an idyllic pond with a partner who is fishing, the aesthetics of the situation eludes us and we may wish we were ashore.

We cannot complete an aesthetic train of thought, or make the connection between a work of art or experience of beauty and an idea. Something is "missing in action" as we look, hear, or read. We say, for example, that the art of Ryoan-ji signifies emptiness; we say that the art of Chartres points to Providence. But the references are ambiguous, nonpersistent, and frequently confusing. Nothing can function as a sign without referring to something else, but that something else is not readily present. At best, there are only traces, fleeting traces—perhaps traces of traces. Sometimes, these traces are just "murmurings," indistinct and incomplete. Jacques Derrida, French philosopher and critic, calls this lack or absence *différance,* inventing a French word more radical than *différence,* meaning not just different, but lacking. Derrida first worked out his theory in *Grammatology,* in which the lack in a statement, a "text," or a work of art was called a "gram." *Différance* and a gram became nearly synonymous. The signified idea is different from the signifier, to be sure, but now any definite connection between the two is called into question. Thoreau, in his observations by Walden Pond, spoke of "severe beauty," a beauty whose meaning is not only harsh, but severely limited in its ability to be understood. Mark C. Taylor, a perceptive interpreter of postmodernist thought, adds an "i" to the word *revelation* to make it "reveilation," or a re-veiling.

Even more crucial, disquiet, lack, absence, disorienting are found in the thing itself, prior to the problem of a connection with an idea. In a text or a work of art, all meaning is indirect and deferred. There is no expert who can give a meaning to a work of art, not even the composer, the poet, the maker. T. S. Eliot wrote, "A recording of a poem read by its author is no more definitive an 'interpretation' than a recording of a symphony conducted by the composer. The poem, if it is of any depth and complexity, will have meanings in it concealed from the author; and should be capable in being read in many ways."[7] But the meanings are endless. In a work of art we are looking deep into something that goes on and on—like the picture of a picture of a picture on a cereal box.

Shigematsu wrote of this insight:

> *Bring the bright moon*
> *into the bottomless*
> *bamboo basket.*
> *Store the clear wind*
> *in the mindless*
> *cup.*[8]

The garden of Ryoan-ji presents itself as an art form without a floor. Before one's eyes, something is being drained away. Sometimes the enormity of Chartres makes one feel so small and insignificant that one has a feeling of slipping through a crack in the floor and falling down and down. This quality of a text and of a work of art Derrida described to a Japanese colleague as being connected with the verb *se déconstruire*, to deconstruct itself. The object viewed loses its construction; its many-faceted qualities all call for attention. It loses its structure; there is nothing, Derrida would say, "logocentric" about it. This deconstruction takes place; it does not wait for the deliberation or consciousness of a viewer. Derrida would have us see that this built-in process delimits ontology, or a theory of being or of completeness. In its very presentation, a work of art "unsays itself."

Both of these approaches exert a claim on us. A thing of beauty has the power of making us at home, of providing orientation, of presenting acceptance, of offering knowable presence. A work of art speaks to us in comforting terms; it displays fullness and being. But, aesthetic theory also points to our disquiet, our anxiety as we try to make a connection with a signified idea or concept. Moreover, the work of art has a many-sided, disparate power that breaks open its own meaning and structure before our eyes and in our seeing. It opens us to ontological incompleteness. It presents absence and non-being.

Presence and being and absence and non-being are related and touch each other. They are not mutually exclusive; each, in a sense, depends upon the other. We would not be attracted to the idea of Providence in Chartres were we not, at the same time, mystified, puzzled, bereft of understanding. Ryoan-ji is not so empty, so blank, that our eye does not find a definite meaning in a certain cluster of rocks. The two qualities lead into each other and are always connected in any work of art. They reciprocally limit each other. Neither one takes over. There may be presence, there may be absence—more likely a combination or overlapping of the two. With respect to our feelings, there may be a gathering in, an "at home"; there may be a scattering, a disorienting.

But, in aesthetics, there is always detail. There is, in a work of art, something angular, particular, singular which catches us, whether any theory of aesthetics or analysis of emotion emerges. Ralph Waldo Emerson wrote, "I ask not for the great, the remote. . . . I embrace the common, I explore and sit at the feet of the familiar, the low. Give me insight into today. . . . What would we really know the meaning of? The meal in the firkin . . . the ballad in the street; the news of the boat; the glance of the eye; the form and gait of the body—show me . . . and the world lies no longer a dull miscellany and a lumber-room."[9] To be sure, Emerson in the working out of his aesthetic theory would speak of "one design uniting," but the beginning of the sense of beauty was in the particular. To concentrate on the detail is to make a radical departure from former aesthetic theory.

Sir Joshua Reynolds, the late eighteenth-century English artist and critic, wrote in *Discourses on Art* that beauty involves rising above singular forms, local customs, particularities, and details. In contrast, following emphases in G. F. Hegel, modern critics, such as Roland Barthes, give their attention to single lines in a drawing, notes, postscripts, mistakes, the angle of a wing in flight. Marxist theories of art hold that an "aesthetic object" can only be described in accordance with its succession of concretizations, understood in the unfolding of social history, but also in the particularities of a work of art. Many argue that the sense of fullness, engulfment, or understanding of being, which fall under the first meaning of aesthetics, can be comprehended first only by the dissimulation into beings or into particulars. And if there is no theory or broad conceptualization possible at all—the point of the second theory—we only have particulars. Frequently, our theories and fabrications get in the way of the details present in an art form. We need to be freed, as many say today, from "His Majesty the Ego" and his constructions.

How much this kind of aesthetic sense is needed in our religious lives! As religious persons and members of worshiping communities we are so often frenetic and vapid. Normative concepts of faith, institutional structures, either/or judgments easily occupy us. Our liturgy, Christian education of our children, our church buildings all too frequently make shallow use of art and its expansive power. In our own personal lives, we all too seldom stop and see—or listen or make or do. We respond inadequately to "O sing to God a new song; sing to God, all the earth. . . . Declare God's glory . . . God's marvelous works among all the peoples" (Ps. 96:1, 3). We do not grasp the power of the details God has placed before us.

Our spiritual life stands in need of the broadest concept of art. Both the partaking and the doing of works of art are part of our spiritual journey. We need to appreciate, understand, and participate in both classical and modern art in all their expressions, remembering that beauty, truth, and goodness are always related. Each can be the doorway into the others. Beauty, therefore, is both the revelation of the presence of goodness or truth, or priestly art (such as Emil Nolde's *Christ among the Children* in plate 7) and the revelation of the absence of goodness or truth, or prophetic art (such as Pablo Picasso's *Guernica,* a result of the first saturation bombing of civilians in the Spanish Civil War, in plate 8).

Most people can and do understand beauty in terms of priestly art. It also represents the art they prefer. Prophetic art is more difficult to understand, affirm, or appreciate. Still, both understandings are necessary and important. Beauty is never without its shadowy side, that which is the distortion of the positive, that which unmasks the evil in the human condition. Those who refuse to gaze upon it or cannot see it deny revelation and can easily brush aside its prophetic realism.

Martin Luther, elaborating his medieval inheritance, spoke of God as *Deus revelatus,* revealed, and *Deus absconditus,* hidden. Luther sensed the fullness and beauty of God in scripture and sacrament. But he also knew the disorienting, shattering power of God in the beauty of the liturgy when, at his first celebration and often afterwards, he felt bereft, broken, empty. In its broadest sense, our search for art of all kinds in our spiritual journey will depend on our acceptance of presence and absence—and our rejoicing in the details.

27

FOR REFLECTION AND DISCUSSION

1. Can you "leave" your own culture and enter into another? How far can you enter? What are some of the problems? The advantages?

2. What particular art form from another culture has "captured" you and why? Native American? Aztec? Other?

3. Can you feel both "at home" with an art form and also disquieted or disoriented by it? Think of some art form that does both. Or is an art experience for you usually one way or the other?

TWO

AESTHETICS AND TRUTH

*Beauty is truth, truth beauty—that is all you know on
earth and all you need to know.*

John Keats

*The earth is God's and all that is in it,
the world, and those who live in it;
for God has founded it on the seas,
and established it on the rivers.*

Psalm 24

PERCEPTION, IMAGINATION, AND IMAGE

Classical Chinese painters were skilled in calligraphy and poetry as
well as in brush and ink painting. All three of these pursuits were
thought to be expressions, primarily, of the beauty of the natural
world—the changes of the seasons, the flow of water, the light shifting on mountains, the movement of tidal rivers. These artists were
known as the *literati* of Chinese culture, a word denoting persons
whose work not only pleased the eye but elevated the soul by the
work's representation of the world of nature. The Tao, or the great
Way, itself is equated with nature. The philosophical twenty-fifth
chapter of the *Tao Te Ching* concludes: "People follow the earth;
earth follows heaven; heaven follows the Tao; the Tao follows the
natural."

The high road of representation, the truth of nature, was
thought to be reserved particularly for painting and other forms of
visual arts. Huang Pin-hung (1864–1955), a modern *literati*
painter who wished to maintain the traditional Chinese form of representing nature rather than imitating Western contemporaries,
spoke of the *ch'i*, energy, of nature that could be presented in painting. Huang spoke of a good painting as being "orderly in its disorder, disorderly in its order; it is totally permeated with dynamic

energy; this energetic flow endows it with an active presence, a musical quality; it is inhabited with a life of its own."[1] The truth of the *ch'i* of nature arose through disciplined, imaginative brush work. *Ch'i* is a quality which comes from the cosmic spirit of nature, so Chinese painters felt. It vitalizes all things—gives movement to water, is exhaled by the mountains as clouds and mist, gives growth to trees in the form of sun and rain, gives energy to people as they coordinate their efforts with natural elements.

In representing the *ch'i* of nature a painter must enter into the energy of the scene being painted. "Become the bamboo!" was advice masters gave their pupils. Chinese painters were known to have dug ink-stained fingers deep into their huge brush so that they might feel the energy of the instrument of representation—before they sought to put on rice paper a landscape or a tree or a bird. Painting had a chance, so this culture believed, of presenting the world of nature in its constant display of energy and change. The visual became a true way of understanding the majesty of the natural world. Poetry could be written about the changes of the seasons and artful calligraphy could describe a mountain range, but painting was a direct way of representing the many-sidedness of nature—and nature's powerful embodiment of supreme truth in the world.

29

The Trinity—the essential dogma of Christian faith, namely, that one God exists in three persons and one substance—can be understood appropriately as an intellectual category, a conviction concerning truth, a statement about the mysterious nature of God. The Trinity can be also understood appropriately as an intuitive category, a communal experience of the truth, a subjective engagement with the mysterious nature of God. The first understanding is served by theology and rational discourse, the second by the visual arts and the imagination. Both are ways of knowing the truth.

Edward Robinson, sculptor and director of the Center for Spirituality and the Arts at Oxford University, defines art as a means of revealing truth through sensuous perception. Aesthetics is the study of perception and its expressions. Often the visual arts are dismissed or ignored as a way of knowing the truth because our understanding of perception is inadequate. Visual thinking, like faith, is one key to knowing and knowledge. Perception is an activity of the mind, an intuitive way of thinking and knowing which calls for the use of images and the imagination to reveal that which is invisible and otherwise inaccessible.

Aesthetic experience emphasizes the sacramentality of life—that within the material or secular is the non-material or sacred and that the sacred can be seen in the secular through the eyes of faith. The artist is aware that the familiar is charged with mystery which explains why aesthetic experience and religious experience have been closely aligned historically.

While truth is a polymorphous concept, truth in every case makes it possible for us to see things as they really are, without distortion or concealment. Insofar as the human quest is for self-understanding and meaning, we humans seek existential truth, for this truth brings to light the meaning and reality of human life. Therefore, it is lived truth in contrast to verbal truth. Theology is first concerned with uncovering our being-in-the-world and only secondarily with statements about propositional truth. Because this is true, the arts precede the science of theology and its attempts to express in language the truth revealed through the arts. It is important, then, for anyone doing theology to be immersed in the arts. Wittgenstein has said that propositions are pictures of reality, but even more so are the visual arts propositions of reality. If we are to know the truth we will need to acquire the eyes of an artist and practice the art of gazing upon art.

There are many ways to see. We can choose to see or not to see. We can see the whole or parts of the whole. We can see directly or indirectly. Further, we always interpret what we see and give meaning to what we are able to see. Two people gazing upon the same sight may see different realities. Two people interpreting what both have seen may find different meanings. Presumably everyone seeks to see clearly or accurately, to see wholly and fully. Still, seeing with our mind's eye and our imagination's eye is conditioned by how we have learned to look and what we have learned to look for.

Aesthetic experience and expression prevent religion from becoming irrelevant; they disengage us from a world of theological concepts and biblical literalism. Aesthetic experience and expression go beneath the surface of the physical world and thereby reveal what is otherwise hidden. Aesthetic experience and expression are concerned with the incarnation of mystery through a way into the nature of beauty and thereby of truth and goodness.

Truth, goodness, and beauty are related to each other. None can be grasped fully by cognitive processes alone. Our deepest truths are noncognitive, rooted in the realm of the imagination. It is not in doctrine but in experience that people encounter God. While doctrine may influence our experience, it is from our experience that doctrine is derived. The visual arts, like faith, provide us with a way to look at life and at our own lives.

Martin Buber wrote, in a classic scheme, about various types of relationships. In an "I–it" relationship the other is an object from which we disengage and distance ourselves, avoiding emotion. In an "I–thou" relationship the other is a subject with which we engage, involving our emotions. A work of art is properly a "thou," a subject to which we relate, not an object which we analyze. Works of art are to be encountered and experienced rather than classified and articulated. To look at Huang Pin-hung's *Rocky Crags and Distant Field at Water's Edge* is to be pulled into a contrasting world of rough rocks and a cultivated field, calling us to enter in with our responses and hard-to-explain feelings (see plate 9). Buber said that the world is not comprehended, but rather embraced.

31

To know about is to conceptualize objectively, but to know is to encounter subjectively. Eastern artists and philosophers often contrast "knowledge" and "knowing." To speak of God is not to talk about God. The Bible is not for the church primarily a literary object to be dissected; it is a revelatory subject to engage us and thereby to reveal to us what we might otherwise miss. Similarly, a work of art needs to be encountered subjectively so that it can engage us and reveal to us what is hidden.

Revelation is at the center of religion and religious experience. Revelation is better approached as an aesthetic than as a scientific category, for it calls for subjective participation and the imagination rather than objective observation and analysis. Emphasis on rationalism during the Enlightenment made the aesthetic inferior and suspect, thereby diminishing the natural ability of persons to be engaged by religious experience. We may have forgotten that all experience need not be expressed as propositions and that some experiences might be better expressed and communicated through the visual arts. Further, we have forgotten that understanding can come from the experience of works of art as well as from the written word. Verbal literacy is necessary but not sufficient. Visual literacy is also important, especially if we are concerned with religious truth.

The psychologist Jerome Bruner has contended that our conception of reality is affected by our seeing. He contrasts the symbolism of the right and the left hand, the doer and thinker with the dreamer and imaginer. The left hand may be awkward, but it points to the creative. Reaching for knowledge with the left hand implies the visual arts. As a right-handed psychologist, he explains that he studied cognitive processes, but by doing so he came to realize their limitations and discovered the significance of the left hand and intuition. Frederick Franck, an artist of Roman Catholic and Zen persuasions, writes about the intuitive power of seeing, contrasted with looking and analyzing. Seeing can become "a way of meditation, a way of getting into intimate touch with the visible world around us, and through it . . . with ourselves."[2]

Children see before they speak. Still, the relationship between what we see and what we know is complex and paradoxical. For example, the way we see is affected by what we know, but what we see affects what we know. We see only what we look at. We can see only what is offered us to see. To reveal is an act of choice, but so is to see what is revealed. An image is a sight re-created or reproduced for us to see. It can influence our seeing, but we may choose either not to look at it or to look at it with prejudice and quick judgment.

Images make present what is absent, but images have a scope and intention, pointing toward and directing us to something. Images can represent what is present in a variety of ways so that we can see more clearly and fully what is present, making possible interpretations that might easily be missed. An image can outlast what can be seen in the present. But images can also limit or distance what we might see, and they can record for all time what was never there in the first place.

As an example, consider the image of the transfiguration, an image often used in worship and meditation in liturgical churches. The experience of this image for both of us comes from our association with the Taizé community, an ecumenical community based in Burgundy, France, whose members have visited American college and university campuses and whose members have taken the vow of poverty while living and working in the slums of Chicago and in Latin American cities. The image is based on the account in Luke 9:28–36 which tells of Jesus' ascent of a mountain, of his garments and face being transformed into a dazzling appearance, and of the sudden appearance of Moses and Elijah. Peter, observing all of this along with John and James, the three being heavy with sleep but awake, said, "Master, it is good for us to be here; let us make three booths, one for you, one for Moses, and one for Elijah." The Taizé image, painted on a small block of wood, easily transported, reproduced, and given to visitors at the community, shows the three booths with Jesus in shining raiment in the middle flanked by Moses and Elijah. The image can be set on a bureau, on a desk, on an altar, on a table between candles in a place of private prayer and meditation.

To see this image of the transfiguration, even for a few moments, is a powerful experience—at least for us. It directs us toward the Christ event; it does have a focus although the lens is wide and offers many lines of sight. Of course, it could be dismissed as a kind of Lukan fantasy about Christ or as a dream the drowsy Peter had while waiting. The way the image is seen depends on our perception of truth about the Christ event. On what can the image focus for those of us who have beliefs, no matter how varied, about the meaning of Christ? It can remind us of Jesus' connection with the law, now presented by the figure of Moses standing on one side, and of Jesus' connection with prophecy, represented by Elijah standing on the other. The image can remind us of the specialness of the incarnation—particularly when we read, after Peter's suggestion about the three dwellings, about the voice coming out of the cloud, "This is my Son, my Chosen; listen to him!" (Luke 9:35).

Seeing the transfiguration in the Taizé image can, in our responses, prefigure the resurrection—a Christ with visage altered and clad in shining white. Perhaps our response, as we see and concentrate, is focused on the dwellings or booths, simple, earthbound shelters for the three, reminding us of the worldly, in-dwelling presence of Moses, Elijah, and Jesus. The dwellings honor the three-

33

some, but they also make the law, the prophecy, and the Word present before our eyes. The image is explosive. The more we concentrate on it the more the focus broadens—and the more there is to be seen and the more there is to know. The transfiguration and other images are to be worked on and struggled with. Images will lead us to ask about our resistance. But as we work and concentrate and let the power of the visual enter our hearts and minds, we may be able to grasp that seeing is a consequence of our starting place, of our knowing and believing, and that our starting place of knowing and believing is expanded and becomes a consequence of our seeing.

The poet John Keats, in a letter to Benjamin Bailey in 1817, wrote, "I am certain of nothing but the holiness of the heart's affections and the truth of the imagination—what the imagination sees as beauty must be truth."[3] But, as in all revelation, we must see what is shown and we must learn to see and to see critically.

A WAY FOR THE CHURCH

In our culture we too easily emphasize words. We say Jesus is the Word of God, but what does that mean? A child says of absent parents, "Ma-Ma, Da-Da," in order to make them present. Words do help to make things present—and so it is with the Word of God, which is Jesus and the life he lived. But we need a sense of what is missing before our words can have any meaning or express a genuine longing. In Christian faith, we must take both the Word and the words seriously, knowing that the Word comes before the words. In the longing of the child, the presence of the parent comes before the words that reveal the absent parent to the child. Catechesis, or learning to be Christian, means literally "echoing the Word." Some people view a catechetical exercise as the mindless repeating of words, that is, of doctrinal assertions. But "echoing the Word" can also mean manifesting the presence and action of the Word, of Jesus. The church is called to be the body of Christ, Christ's presence and action in the world; to be the icon of the Word, a visual image of the Word, for all the world to see and experience. Truth is a visual manifestation, the aesthetic of truth. Faith as belief in the truth, as the attitude of trusting in the truth, as doing the truth are valuable constructs. But faith is best understood as perception, as the seeing of the truth which is to be believed in, trusted in, and acted upon.

Iconography is art for the church. It is intended to aid faith as perception and by so doing support revelation, that is, our seeing the truth. It is the gift of sight to the blind. We all need help to see the truth. The church aids us by presenting images for us to gaze upon. These images inform, inspire, guide, encourage, and illumine the faithful.

The faith of the church is in what we cannot see on our own. The art of the church gives us help with to our seeing. Seeing, as we have discussed, is a complex process. When we dream we see. When we stare we see. When we close our eyes we see. The more important issue is: To what do we pay attention? Do we ignore our dreams, stare only at television, and refuse to look at the visual arts? We are responsible for what we choose to see.

Icons—flat pictures, usually painted by a religious person in a time of meditation, in oil on wood but also wrought in mosaic, ivory, or other materials, to represent religious subjects—ask us to gaze, to give them our complete attention. Their purpose is to offer us access, through the gate of the visible, to the mystery of the invisible. Like a sacrament, they are an outward and material sign of an inward and spiritual reality.

Zen Buddhists and their Western friends face an impossible task of explaining or comprehending the meaning of *sunyata,* emptiness, but when they sit on the veranda of the rock and stone garden of Ryoan-ji in Kyoto they sense in the simplicity and calmness the meaning of letting go and casting aside. The garden offers them an opportunity for perceiving a central Buddhist idea. Before *zazen,* or formal meditation, Zen teachers often suggest that pupils concentrate on a Taoist or Zen painting which presents in its composition a meaning of *sunyata.* To "see into" a painting of an unfilled, hazy valley with indistinct mountains in the far background and to see the calligraphy on the side, for example, is to prepare one for the emptiness of *zazen.* The function of religious expression is to illumine the truth and draw us deeper into life's depth. In making incarnate our human experience of mystery, wonder, and awe, the arts help us encounter the sacred or holy. Without the visual arts we are cut off from our most important means into truth, for "the sym-

35

bol gives rise to the thought," as philosopher Paul Ricoeur and others have said. Truth and the aesthetic go hand in hand.

While the Western church's art is dominated by the Passion, the way of the cross, the Eastern church's art, the icon, is dominated by the great feast of Christ, the reign of God. Images of the crucifixion in the West reveal a martyr undergoing an act of agony; in the East the crucifixion reveals the triumph of the cross. The resurrection in the West is a transformation from death into glory, but in the East it is Christ's descent into hell for universal redemption of the world. Clearly we need both emphases. Our art reveals our understanding of and convictions about the truth of the Christ event.

One of the early representations of Christ in Christian art depicts a crucified human figure with the head of an ass. Intellectual debate on its meaning continues, but perhaps the catacomb Christians had a deep sense of the cosmic absurdity of their intellectual position. They must have sensed how ludicrous their claims of truth appeared. It was irrational and illogical. Christ was for them a holy fool, and they knew they were fools for Christ. Herbert Marcuse and other contemporary philosophers have insisted that we need to break the power of facts over the world and find a language which is not the language of those who establish, enforce, coerce, and benefit on the basis of such facts. Those foolish Christians could speak the broken language; they had faith and hope in the eternal foolishness of God whose truth was in the imagination and could never be seen except through the eyes of faith.

Elliot Eisner in *Education as Artistic Vision* explains that the visual arts deal with an aspect of human consciousness that no other field touches—the aesthetic contemplation of truth. Lionel Trilling in *Beyond Culture* states that art yields more than any other activity by revealing not only the commonplace, but the deepest human aspirations, hopes, and fears that may be apprehended and comprehended. The visual arts are at the frontier of our knowledge of ourselves.

Human life depends on our ability to image, to picture both accurately and imaginatively. We can deceive ourselves as to the truth if we do not image well. F. A. Kenkule, the chemist who discovered the benzene ring, urges us to learn to imagine—and then perhaps we shall discover the truth (see plate 10—the angel Gabriel appears to Mary as a column of light). Does this perhaps explain why from the dawn of human existence there has been art? Regretfully, we have made truth into an intellectual category and overrationalized religion. Is it any wonder that our age suffers from an impaired consciousness? It is not so much that we have overemphasized the intellectual (anti-intellectualism is still alive and well); it is just that we have denied the intuitive, the visual way into the truth and thereby limited our access to the truth. The church is concerned with both; the Christian is to do the truth. In our day, to discover the truth, to experience the truth, to manifest the truth for others to see, will call for a new concern for the commitment to aesthetics, the intuitive way of thinking and knowing, the visual arts, and the imagination.

FOR REFLECTION AND DISCUSSION

1. What painting or art form has shown you the ch'i, energy, of nature? Has it brought you closer to a basic concept or truth about nature?

2. Has a tenet of Christian faith been made more acceptable and understandable to you by an art form—for example, the creation of humankind by God, as in Michelangelo's painting of God reaching down to touch Adam's finger on the Sistine Chapel ceiling in Rome? the Trinity? the resurrection?

3. In responding to an art form, how has your imagination led you closer to an understanding of Christian truth?

THREE

AESTHETICS AND GOODNESS

*That which is beautiful . . . has a generally extended
excellence and a true beauty; and the more extended
or limited its system is, the more confined or extended
is its beauty.*

Jonathan Edwards, Notes on the Mind

*The "Hua-yen" sutra refines our understanding of . . .
interpenetration: that I and all beings perfectly reflect
and indeed are all people, animals, plants. . . . The
metaphor is the "Net of Indra," a model of the universe
in which each point of the net is a jewel that perfectly
reflects all other jewels.*

Robert Aitken, The Mind of Clover: Essays in Zen Buddhist Ethics

38

In the *Nicomachean Ethics* Aristotle asks the question: What is the relation of insight to action? The question is similar to an issue raised by Plato in the *Republic:* What is the relation of art to politics? To answer generally: The extent and the energy of aesthetics do spill over into what we do in life and help determine the direction and content of our actions. Of course, an "aesthete" may be considered as one who withdraws, lives a private and reclusive life, and stops short of answering Aristotle's and Plato's questions. Kitaro Nishida, the Japanese Zen philosopher, states the wider view by claiming that our response to beauty, known in both fullness and emptiness, "passes over into things" and helps to govern our responses and responsibilities.

In this chapter we offer the reader some links between aesthetics and ethics. Insofar as beauty can be the revelation of goodness, it is understandable that a friend of ours, hearing about this project, remarked, "The most beautiful thing in the world to me was Mother Teresa's face." Compassion and giving in action open an-

PLATE 1

Georges Rouault, *Christ Crowned with Thorns*, 20th-century French

(© 1998 Artists Rights Society (ARS), N.Y./ADAGP, Paris)

(see page 9)

PLATE 2

Ue Gukei, *Fisherman with Nets,*
14th-century Chinese

(see page 10)

PLATE 3

Chartres (approach across grain fields), medieval Gothic cathedral southwest of Paris (courtesy of Williams College Art Department)

PLATE 4

Chartres (west exterior), medieval Gothic cathedral southwest of Paris (courtesy of Williams College Art Department)

(see pages 15 and 16)

PLATE 5

Japanese Zen temple (approach through the maples), Kyoto, Japan

(see page 16)

PLATE 6
Ryoan-ji, Zen rock
and stone garden,
Kyoto, Japan
(*see page 17*)

PLATE 7
Emil Nolde, *Christ among the Children*, 1910, German, oil on canvas, 34 1/8" x 41 7/8", (© 1998 The Museum of Modern Art, N.Y.)

(*see page 27*)

PLATE 8

Pablo Picasso,
Guernica, 20th-century
Spanish (© 1998 Estate
of Pablo Picasso/
Artists Rights Society
(ARS), N.Y.)

(see page 27)

PLATE 9

Huang Pin-hung, *Rocky Crags and Distant Field at Water's Edge,*
20th-century Chinese

(see page 31)

PLATE 10

Henry O. Tanner, *The
Annunciation*, 1898, North
American (used by permission
of The Philadelphia
Museum of Art, the
W. P. Wilstach Collection)
(*see page 37*)

PLATE 11

John Singer Sargent, *Carnation, Lily, Lily, Rose,*
19th-century North American (used by permission of the
Tate Gallery, London/Art Resource, N.Y.)

The photograph of girls playing in the garden with Chinese lanterns is an
excellent example of inviting, suggestive, imaginative yin.

(see page 53)

PLATE 12

Mu-chi, *Kingfisher*, medieval Chinese

(see page 56)

PLATE 13

Ma Lin, *Sunset*, medieval Chinese

(see page 70)

PLATE 14

Samuel Parker Armstrong (8-year-old grandson of John Dykstra Eusden),

Stained Glass Window in My Church That I Look At

(see page 81)

PLATE 15

Liang Kai, *Shakyamuni Descending the Mountain,* medieval Chinese

(see page 90)

PLATE 16

Pieter Brueghel the
Elder, *The Census
at Bethlehem*,
16th-century Flemish
(used by permission
of Scala/Art
Resource, N.Y.)
(*see page 90*)

PLATE 17

Ryokan Daigu, *Heaven and Earth,* 19th-century Japanese

(see page 93)

other door into the meaning of aesthetics. Mother Teresa's gaunt, wrinkled, tired face spoke of unflagging caring and service. Her commitment and life struggles put together goodness and the beautiful. Watching her eyes, observing her small, bent body, and hearing her tell of her work among the poor in spirit as well as in substance, whether the outcasts of Calcutta or prisoners in America, one grasped a meaning of the beautiful.

BEAUTY AND ETHICS

Jonathan Edwards (1703–1758), the preacher of the religious revival known as the Great Awakening and probably America's most influential theologian, was captured by the idea of beauty. Moving beyond his Calvinist roots, which stressed God's sovereignty and power, Edwards saw God involved in what was to Edwards the first metaphysical principle, known as being. God was not the One beyond being, but the exemplifier through beauty of the meaning of being itself. God and being project together into our lives. In his *Nature of True Virtue* and *Religious Affections,* Edwards spoke of being as the lifefulness and energy which pervade the world. God is to be known in the beautiful "absolute space" of the cosmos where lifefulness and energy reside.

39

Ethics is concerned with the visions people live by. It is concerned with what people see. To extend Jonathan Edwards's thought, consider the Neur, an African tribe, who believe that if a child is born with a disability it is not a child but a hippopotamus. That is, they do not see a human life, but a hippo. They name the life accordingly and, believing that hippos belong in the river, place the life in the water, where it ultimately drowns. From their perspective that action is neither murder nor euthanasia. Before we judge the Neur, it would be well for us to be aware of the ways we do the same. Our enemy in a war is never a human being; the criminal we intend to kill through judicial murder (capital punishment) is called an animal; the fetus we intend to kill through medical murder (abortion) is not a child, but unwanted tissue. Our ways of seeing and perceiving determine our naming and thereby influence our deciding and acting.

The problem, of course, is complex. During a visit to Germany, while gazing at the idyllic beauty of the Bavarian Alps from a hotel window one morning, one of us pondered the question: How could Hitler grow up looking at these beautiful mountains every day and turn out as he did? An old Bavarian priest in a subsequent conversation commented on the artistic rendering of space inside the churches—an architectural plan that shared a similar idyllic, otherworldly beauty. He commented that perhaps Hitler and the people who followed him grew up looking only at the ideal and in their pathology set out to eliminate anything or anyone they believed did not fit it. In one Bavarian Alps hotel, there are many paintings that Hitler commissioned to be painted over so that viewers would only see idealistic images of nature and not the more realistic images of people, pictured in their work, their life situation, their struggles.

Jonathan Edwards saw beauty apprehended directly by "immediate sensation" rather than indirectly by reflection. It is by direct sensation or immediate experience of an object's beauty or deformity that the object is understood. There is a difference, Edwards asserts, between mere speculative rational response to an object and its true beauty. The reason is that the former rests solely in the head, while the latter includes the heart. The difference between deciding on the basis of reason that something is beautiful and having a direct sensual experience of its beauty is crucial in the determination of the will. The attractive power will be liveliest when the "manner of view" is sensual rather than speculative alone, for if we make a rational judgment that something is beautiful without any sensibility to its beauty or any feeling about it, we will not necessarily choose it.

According to Edwards, God and beauty are present in creation together, and each can be known through the other. In Jesus Christ, God is present as an object of sensibility in whom beauty is manifest and able to be grasped. Further, God is presented subjectively or inherently as the beauty of holiness, of spiritual sensibility. Edwards presents this kind of beauty as the Holy Spirit. The good in God in Christian living is conceived before us as the beauty of Jesus and in us as the beauty of the Holy Spirit. Beauty, then, in Edwards's theology, becomes the measure of goodness and the highest good.

God is distinguished from all other beings in that there is beauty in God's very essence. It is out of God's beauty that creation proceeds; it is by God's beauty that creation is ordered; it is according to God's beauty that God governs the world; it is through God's beauty that God redeems. Beauty provides the model for the Christian life as seen in God's reign among us and in God's promises to us, in which beauty is perfected or fulfilled. Beauty is the mark of both God's transcendence and God's immanence. Insensibility or imperceptiveness to the divine beauty is one way of defining evil, understood as sin and alienation from God.

A person's highest vocation, according to Edwards, is to respond to the beauty of being which God exemplifies and makes possible. One may respond to the harmony, proportion, and majesty of beauty in the world and in the Christian scheme—this Edwards called a secondary or a "natural" form of response. Edwards saved his discussion of primary response to beauty for a "new spiritual sense" which saw aesthetics reaching out to ethics. In eighteenth-century language, beauty is the "cordial and affectional consent of being to being." All persons and things, or all beings, have their place. The majesty and power of God are manifested in God's display and creation of this multiplicity.

For Edwards, the most significant meaning of aesthetics occurs when one being gives assent to, or accepts, another being. A positive response to divergences and differences is beauty in action. The new spiritual sense of which Edwards wrote entails not only cognitive but affectional acceptance—mind and heart reaching out together. Multiple beings make for wonder and "excellence" in Edwards's thought. Out of this excellence come the unity and the connections of the world which God displays and makes possible. Excellence in diversity and the acceptance of it lead to unity, not the other way around. Unity is not a given, not a first principle.

Edwards even saw the political order as a kind of beauty. A good body politic emerges when people commit themselves to the plurality of humanness. Politics can be thought of as a metaphoric or symbolic space. There can be no dissolving of conflictual elements, but the political order looks to the conceptual and affectional consent to differences as a measure of its well-being.

Edwards never saw the task as being easy. Will, dedication, and insight are required; aesthetics arises in the act of beautifying rather than in discovery of the beautified. Roland DeLattre's writing on

41

Jonathan Edwards has probed imaginatively into the "ethics connection" in Edwards's aesthetics.[1]

A strong connection with Confucianism is present, for the *Analects* and other Chinese classics speak of the beauty of the *li*, known as the proper rites, ceremonies, and actions between people. Gestures and responses become aesthetic when good relationships are made between people and acceptance and responsiveness are manifest and vibrant. To "do the fitting in the circumstances," as H. Richard Niebuhr and others have stated, is both an aesthetic and an ethical act.

VISIONING

In modern times, faith has been understood as doctrine, beliefs have been stated as propositional truth. A more historic understanding is faith as perception, a particular way of "seeing" life and our lives— or a worldview that determines our way of living. Since the seventeenth century, we have gradually turned human beings into thinkers and actors, making ethics into decision making and right action, neglecting character and the centrality of vision for the ethical life.

42

Perhaps the moral life can once again be understood as an aesthetic mode of seeing and beholding, rather than only in terms of decision and action. As Amos Wilder writes, "It is at the level of the imagination that the fateful issue of our new world experience must be mastered. . . . Before the message there must be the vision . . . before the prose, the poem."[2]

Alasdair MacIntyre's *After Virtue* provides the stimulus for some Christian ethicists to redirect the focus of their work. Among those most influenced is Stanley Hauerwas, whose work *Character and Virtue* remains a seminal work in the "new ethics." For Hauerwas, to be a Christian is to have one's character or dispositions act in predictable, consistent ways determined in accordance with God's action in Jesus Christ. The aim of the Christian life becomes the acquiring of a vision of God's presence and action in human life and history, rather than the acquisition of the ability to make autonomous, correct choices of right actions. For Hauerwas the key to our behavior is located in our perceptions of life and our lives. Persons differ not because they comprehend a situation differently and have reasoned logically to different conclusions, but because their different experiences have shaped their perceptions differently—that is, they see the world differently. The moral life, therefore, is more than thinking clearly and making a logical choice; it is a way of seeing the world. The moral life is better understood through the analogy of the aesthetic mode of seeing, beholding, and visioning than in terms of analyses, decisions, and actions.

Iris Murdoch, best known for her novels, has in her substantial work on ethics stressed vision. In her book *The Sovereignty of Good,* she argues that art provides the best clue to the nature of the good. She writes, "We can see beauty itself in a way in which we cannot see goodness itself. I can *experience* the transcendence of the beautiful, but (I think) not the transcendence of the good. Beautiful things contain beauty in a way in which good acts do not exactly contain good, because beauty is partly a matter of the senses. So if we speak of good as transcendent we are speaking of something rather more complicated and which cannot be experienced, even when we see the unselfish man in the concentration camp."[3]

Hauerwas, commenting on Iris Murdoch in *Vision and Virtue,* defends the close connection between art and morals. "Good art, unlike bad art or random occurrences, exists over against us in such a way that we must surrender to its authority. Both love and great art show us our world with a clarity that startles us because we are not used to looking at the real world at all. Art, whether representational or not, reveals to us aspects of our world that we are usually too dependent on conventionality and fantasy to be able to see."[4] Art reveals to us that which is hidden from view; it shows to us how different the world and our lives can look. It enlarges our consciousness, enlivens our imaginations, shapes our characters, and forms our perceptions of life or faith.

The moral life is more a matter of attention than of will. We become good by training our attention on the good. Moral goodness requires discipline and training to overcome the many illusions we hold, which come from accepting our culture's perceptions of life and our lives, from conforming to the secular material-rational way of perceiving the world. The moral life, then, does not consist in just making one right decision after another, it is the progressive attempt to widen and clarify our vision of reality.

43

Christian life implies learning "to see" the world through the eyes of God, to attend to the world under the mode of the divine. Christians see the truth and slowly become what they see. To be a Christian means one needs to see life as it is, knowing that vision will influence our character or moral orientation and therefore our direction in life.

In the fifteenth century, there was a growing desire among the faithful to gaze upon Christ, whose life they were to emulate. In time, a devotion known as the benediction, or blessing, of the blessed sacrament evolved, following the liturgy of vespers. Also, persons attended mass and communed by gazing at the consecrated host rather than consuming it. With the Reformation era, a new emphasis emerged, replacing the former age of faith, with its emphasis on "seeing," with a concentration on reading and hearing.

Caleb Gattegno in *Towards a Visual Culture* contends that television is returning sight to a place of significance in our lives. This has been the experience of one of us who has witnessed many parishes desiring to attend the benediction of the blessed sacrament again. While singing the great hymn by Thomas Aquinas, "Humbly I adore thee, Verity unseen," a receptacle called a montsrance containing the consecrated host is placed on the altar so that the congregation kneeling can meditate on this sacrament as an icon and thereby become aware of Christ's presence in their midst. As they do, they say prayers of intercession for all the needy so that Jesus, whom they have come before, will bring those persons to them, so that they, kneeling, might be a sign of his redeeming love.

CAN ART BE "USEFUL"?

In September 1987, a Santa Fe artist, Dominique Mazeaud, commenced an art project entitled *The Great Cleansing of the Rio Grande River*. On a monthly basis—sometimes more often—she and her friends meet to clean trash and pollution from the river. The findings are brought back and arranged in designs, usually as an outdoor exhibit: pieces of broken glass, a little girl's shoes, shiny and dull pieces of metal, crates, a $5 bill.

Dominique Mazeaud has written and spoken about her work on the art project. The collection of objects, the arrangement and display, the practice of keeping a journal about the project are all part of her *praxis,* her "way" or discipline in the project. Sometimes the weather is harsh, but she and others always put in their day on the river. Picking up endless trash, she sees her work as more than a discipline—a way of prayer, like doing countless rosaries. Noting that water is a very sacred symbol in all religions, she observes that we are separated from the waters of life and challenges us to really see our troubled waters—the dead fish floating, the toxic dumping.

The Brazilian artist Bene Fonteles has long been concerned with the connection between his art, music, and poetry projects and the environment. In the main square of Cuiaba, the capital of a western Brazilian state on the border of Bolivia and the Amazon, he brought back the garbage and refuse which weekend picnickers had left in forest and waterfall areas. The refuse was arranged in a shocking display in the square. With other artist friends, Fonteles is a founder of the Mato Grosso Ecological Society, whose purpose is to help establish a nature preserve in the magnificent wilderness area just outside Cuiaba. Fonteles, like Mazeaud, uses and practices his art in a reverential way. Their art has a dramatic sense of purpose.[5] The Jungian psychoanalyst James Hillman has said that the world does not ask for belief; it asks for noticing, attention, application, and care.

45

The work of these and other artists stands in contrast to the common view that art exists only for its own sake, that it has no ethical overtones, that an artist is free from any concept of a compassionate or responsible action. In the work of Mazeaud, Fonteles, and others there is a breaking away from the prevailing patriarchal aesthetic tradition which proclaims the independence, arbitrariness, and self-indulgence of the artist. In the case of these artists and the movement they represent, there is a creative relationship with a feminine archetype which sees a nurturing role for art and artists.

EASTERN VISIONING IN INDRA'S NET

In Hinduism, the god Indra is known in the *Rig-Veda* literature as a celestial sovereign, or "king of the gods." His prominence came in the pre-500 B.C.E. period, during which time his sovereignty was not unlike that of Zeus or Wotan in the West. From his place in the sky he wielded the thunderbolt. He also founded the sun and bestowed life, light, and fertility in the world. He participated enthusiastically in celebrations and drank of the *soma,* an intoxicant from a leafless vine, often without restraint. Later his power and authority were either taken over by or made possible through the work of Vishnu and Shiva. Indra's place and influence among the Vedic gods or divine energies continue in the early history of Buddhism. His kingly role is found in legends that assert his closeness to the Buddha. He is the one who leads in other gods to worship the Buddha at various moments in the Buddha's life. One account stresses his elevated status, recording that he is the one who conducts all other beings into the final worship of the Buddha in the death scene.

Indra is probably most venerated in the Hindu tradition because he is the supreme god of the royal warriors, or the *kisatriyas.* He offers weapons to his followers and uses them himself; among them are bows and arrows and, particularly, a net. It is the weapon of the net which Mahayana Buddhism, the later dominant strand in China and Japan, imaginatively and forcefully portrays. The *Hua-yen Sutra,* a major text of a Buddhist school which arose in China during the T'ang dynasty, 618–907, describes this net in aesthetic terms, hardly ever in references to war or struggle. At each crossing of the net, or at each "eye," there is a single glittering jewel, diamonds alternating with sapphires. Nets of beautiful strands and reflecting jewels are hung in some Hindu temples, where they are worshiped—illumined by candles and gazed upon while chanting.

But the beauty of the net has a meaning beyond worship and liturgy. In one Mahayana account, Indra casts his net over the whole world. The net stretches out infinitely in all directions as it is thrown over the cosmos and all conceivable worlds. The sparkling jewels, the net unfurling, the motion of throwing are aspects of the beautiful in the Indra story. Each jewel has its own identity, known by its color and shape, but each also reflects all the other jewels. Form and substance appear in the blue of the sapphire and emptiness and clarity in the diamond. Together they glitter and sparkle, producing a never-ending reflection. When one looks at a single jewel it appears to have the depth of the sapphire and the emptiness of the diamond as it catches the reflection of all others. Indra's net displays the Hua-yen insistence on *dharma-dhartu,* mutual identity and mutual dependence, or intercausality. The net-in-motion displays a universe to be known in its dynamism and interrelationships.

Indra casts his net, and it is thought to be the beautiful in action. What does it do? It draws all things together. People are pulled together in the casting and the gathering of the net. Indra throws his beautiful net in a beautiful motion to draw the whole world together. Third-person entities—she, he, it, they—become I and me. Under the net, as Dogen, the medieval Japanese Soto Zen teacher, put it strongly, "Others are none other than myself." In the translated term of Keiji Nishitani, the net is "circuminsessional," or a field of force linking all things together. The jewels are beautiful, the throwing is graceful, but the point of the story is to bring us shoulder to shoulder and heart to heart—to reflect and relate to each other as diamonds and sapphires do. To afford us a vision of one world.

FOR REFLECTION AND DISCUSSION

1. Describe any piece of art that has moved you to behave in a new way, or do something of value for others.

2. Jonathan Edwards (1703–1758) saw a "primary meaning" of beauty occur when assent to and acceptance of others who are different take place. Have such "beautiful events" ever occurred in your life?

3. Like Indra's net, has any art form spoken to you about people and things being truly connected?

II

Aesthetics and
the Human Spirit

F O U R

HUMAN LIFE AND WHOLENESS

The night is far gone,
the day is near.
Let us then lay aside the works of the night
and put on the armor of light.

Romans 13:12

Be really whole,
And all things will come to you.

Tao Te Ching, chapter 22

IMAGINATION—THE YIN IN OUR LIVES

Art requires and releases a discipline of vision so that we learn to look differently into the heart of human life. Such looking shifts our whole way of reading the significance of the world. In its wake, we find our own existence reshaped from the experience of what we have seen.

51

Perhaps it takes a philosopher of art who is herself a writer of imaginative fiction to show how such experience actually shapes the lives of human beings. In her novel *The Bell*, Iris Murdoch narrates a visit by Dora to the National Gallery in London. In earlier sections of the novel the moral and emotional challenge of Dora's world has been transformed into the stuff of fantasy by her "destructive trance-like solipsism." But that is quite set aside by a moment in the art gallery. The artworks before her bestow on her a sense of reality beyond herself, and the experience is spoken of in terms of a seeming revelation.

"The painting spoke to her kindly, yet in sovereign tones," and Dora felt that she had an overwhelmingly new insight. "She looked at the radiant somber power in a canvas of Gainsborough and felt a sudden desire to go down on her knees before it, embracing it, shedding tears. . . . She gave a last look at the painting still smiling as one might smile in a temple favored, encouraged, and loved." It occurred to Dora that perhaps here at last was something revealing, something perfect. "She wonders who had said that, about perfect and reality being in the same place?"[1]

Rudolf Arnheim in *Visual Thinking* opened up the word "perception" so that it means much more than that which is received by the senses when stimulated by the environment. Art provides a form of thinking and knowing, a mode of consciousness and an activity of the mind. Perceptual thinking is not irrational, nor is it fired by undisciplined whim and fancy. It uses all the faculties, urging us to a wider meaning of understanding.

A familiar rendition of the two hemispheres of the brain by popular science has these two functions divided. The right hemisphere which controls the left side of the body, thinks intuitively; the left hemisphere, which controls the right side of the body, thinks intellectually. This theory of the two distinctive roles for the hemisphere is highly disputed by scholars and neurologists. The brain is far more complex and integrated than popular science would have us believe. Certainly, the signals crossing between the two hemispheres are a matter of discussion and of quandary; whether a person is left-handed or right-handed produces a different ascription of qualities to the hemispheres.

It appears that some people may have greater potential for one function over the other and that a culture may value one more than the other and therefore nurture its development to the detriment of the other. Understanding the function of the mind is further complicated by discoveries that humans may have multiple aptitudes or intelligences such as linguistic, logical, mathematical, musical, body-kinesthetic, interpersonal, intrapersonal, and spatial, any one of which a culture may establish as having greater value and therefore encourage.

To know, to prove, to argue is to break in and take apart, bespeaking an aggressive act implying conquest; such a mode treats truth as an object of investigation. On the other hand, to apprehend, to attain, to look for contiguity is to let in and appreciate. Such a mode is a nonaggressive act implying respect. It treats truth as a subject of relationship. Respectively, the two forms are like the yang and yin of Taoist and Confucian thought. The seeds of each are within us, just as are the hemispheres of our brain. Our culture, and many others in the Western world, have tended to emphasize investigation, proof, final definition—or the yang. Art emphasizes the yin mode and urges receptivity, appreciation, and acceptance (see plate 11).

At the core of our humanness is a capacity for the symbolic transformation of experience. Any explanation of human uniqueness must describe and account for this capacity. From the dawn of human existence, humans have made art. Yet all the evidence of our age-old aesthetic sense and our seeming compulsion to make art have not affected our thinking about human beings. It is true that C. G. Jung, early in the 1900s, suggested that creativity is one of the five primary instincts in human beings, but this view is not widely accepted. We humans do have a need to externalize internal images, to communicate personal experience, to give expression to the imagination, to find meaning through symbolization. Still, in spite of all evidence of the human compulsion to create representational symbolic images, our general operative theory of human nature and human needs ignores this aspect of life.

Psychology, for the most part, assumes that human development leads naturally and rightfully to a final state of scientific thinking. Perhaps we need, in our study of our own humanness, a greater awareness of the limits of cognitive theory. Art is taught as history and philosophy, or as practice for those for whom it is a career choice— but rarely do art courses resolve the search for humanness.

Only if the affections are taken seriously will persons have those experiences in education and worship that make religious perceptions possible. Only through the use of the imagination will we gain the insights necessary to give human life broader meaning. We have too often limited our human capacities, neglected our deep consciousnesses, and estranged ourselves from our creative potential through our neglect of the visual arts.

Sir Herbert Read, the philosopher and art critic, advocated that the arts be regarded as the core around which the curriculum of education be built and from which other curriculum concerns might be derived. The visual arts, he contended, need to play a

53

much more significant role in all education, but particularly in religious education. Life in the spirit necessitates a commitment to the visual arts and the intuitive, affective mode of consciousness.

One of the perennial questions in any culture concerns the nature of human beings. Our culture is predispositioned to image humanness in terms of adulthood defined as being independent, rational, and productive. Children, being dependent, nonrational, and nonproductive, are expected to develop or mature, implying adult characteristics. Older persons who do not manifest adult characteristics are considered immature.

In his book *Unfinished Man and the Imagination* Ray Hart envisions the human capacity to image as that which makes it possible for us to both manifest and continually create who we are. Still, the imagination is often regarded with suspicion and is commonly confused with fantasy. Nevertheless, what fundamentally distinguishes us from other species is the ability to image things as being different from what they are. All other animals appear to be programmed to carry on much as they always have, without a past or a future—or without necessarily envisioning a change.

54

The imagination makes it possible for us to move beyond immediate rational explanations that accord with some prevailing philosophical system. To use the imagination is to give free play to a childlike capacity which during the normal development of adolescence and adulthood can easily be lost. If it is not redeveloped at a later time, certain ways of knowing and certain experiences, such as the meaning of revelation and the experience of the presence of God, become increasingly difficult, and we may be left with an understanding of revelation as a doctrine—or, more likely, as a philosophical conclusion that there is no god to be experienced or that we cannot know whether there is or is not, so there is no use in making the effort.

An image can be a symbolic representation, a visual impression, a mental picture, an embodiment of an experience, an expression of an affection. The imagination, the power to form images, is often depreciated in our culture. We dismiss people who engage in it by saying that they are *only* imagining something. We say to a child, "It is all in your imagination"—therefore unreal. Still, Christian piety, that discipline attending to the presence and activity of God, the ability to pray and meditate on scripture, is dependent on the use of the imagination.

The imagination is not a particular faculty of the mind, but a posture of the whole person toward experience. The fact that for many people the experience of God is rare is not a result of God's absence, but of the atrophy of the imagination. When we image, we see beyond the commonsense world, the here and now, the surface appearance of reality. We are not just creatures who think analytically and logically. We have a capacity to exercise this posture of the whole person toward experience—to think intuitively as well as intellectually, to know tacitly as well as explicitly. We have the ability to look into a deeper meaning of our experience. We see this in the natural religiosity of young children and in the mentally disabled. It also explains why religion was expressed in art as images long before it was expressed in words as beliefs.

Imaging, again, is not the same as fantasizing. To use the imagination involves using what a culture, a history, a tradition have presented. Imaging places one within a definite context. Fantasy often tries to break out and leave the person without roots and without necessary cultural configurations. In the language of semiotics, fantasy is the separation from the signifier—meaning that one who fantasizes is unable to connect with the very action or instrumentality by which meaning can be expressed.

In the highly visual culture of medieval Russia, the word for *education, Obrazovanie,* suggests "becoming like the forms, the images." In this sense, there is a certain priority granted to the work of art, the artistic image, over the conscious effort of the perceiver to grasp the vision it holds out. The art is an ontological event and hence cannot be properly understood as an object of aesthetic deliberation. Rather, it is to be grasped in its own ontological structure, for in it being becomes meaningfully visible.

How can we spring our imagination, how can we engage more meaningfully in imaging, how can we use perceptual thinking? How can we be more aware of the yin in our yang-oriented lives?

CONFIDENCE IN THE PRESENT

Thoreau spoke about honoring each moment, lest one damage something larger. His advice is never to give up on the meaning and insight contained in each instant. To give up—or to wait or to reject—is to act "as if you could kill time without injuring eternity."[2] Nishitani Keiji speaks about an insight, a concept, or an interpretation as understandings which arise quickly and then depart. They are "spots" in our awareness and consciousness which we "run quickly across."[3]

In the Japanese tea ceremony, a delicate painting or a few pieces of calligraphy will usually be hung on the wall behind the tea server and celebrant. One which is often used is *hana sho sho*. It means, literally, "flowers here and there." The deeper reference is to the meaning of beauty itself, namely, that beautiful things are everywhere—often in small clusters, often not readily recognized, often in the simplest of arrangements. The call is to the immediacy of an experience—trying to make connections with what one observes and sees in the very moment. There will be more emerging, but start now with what you see.

If one allows oneself to plunge into the immediacy of an artistic presentation, one may begin to see connections, expansions, interpretations taking place in the energy of the moment. In Muchi's famous painting of a kingfisher, one can look directly at the perched bird, but one can also hear in imagination the haunting cry of the kingfisher and the whirring of its wings as it prepares to dive (see plate 12). Perceptual thinking used at the moment presents us with the wholeness of the kingfisher. We sense a possibility of extension or expanding form in ourselves as we engage in the imaginative moment.

READINESS

To prepare for the power of imagination and to allow the yin side of our lives to be present is not easy. It requires a practice and a "way." There is such a thing as "practiced abandonment" before an artwork. The anonymous medieval author of the *Cloud of Unknowing* suggests letting go of "everywhere" and "everything" and exchanging them for "nowhere" and "nothing." The advice continues: Do not worry if you cannot understand this nothing. It is in itself so worthy a thing that no thinking about it will do it justice. This nothing may be felt more than it can be seen.

A practice of observing, contemplating, "standing still before" is not dissimilar to practices in other parts of our lives. In marriage and in all close, intimate relationships, goodness and fulfillment may not always be present. It is true that we promise to love and honor each other, and that we promise to give and receive good things to and from each other, but above all we practice our way of marriage or way of closeness. In the midst of twists and turns, we create a work of art together in our connection. The beginning is not precise, the end is not known, the results are not clear, but the practice is always before us.

To engage in a practice of finding the beautiful, our awareness and alertness must be tuned. In the rush of our frenetic lives, we walk by things or run through them. Many are the Zen temple gardens which are walked by, unobserved by hurrying visitors. How shall a small, delicate thing speak to and through our frantic ways? As Shakespeare wrote in Sonnet 65:

> *How with this rage shall beauty hold a plea,*
> *Whose action is no stronger than a flower?*

The right side of the brain bids us stop, and the yin calls through our yang ways. To answer this bidding and to hear this call require a way and a practice of stopping and beholding.

MYSTERY

An artwork has its own energy and lifefulness and is not beholden to our probes for meaning. We shall not know it all, no matter how great our practice or how deep our attraction. Like the great Way of Taoism, "However fast you run after it, you will never catch it; however fast you run away from it, you will never lose it."[4] The power, or the *te*, of an artwork is its inability to be totally grasped, yet at the same time it exerts a claim upon us. It should be allowed to speak to us in the terms of its own presentation. For similar reasons St. Dionysius preached that the most godlike knowledge of God is that which is known by unknowing. The power of an artwork is like that description of God found in the traditional Hebrew melody Leoni or Yigdal, "The spirit floweth free, high surging where it will."

A Japanese *sumi-e* (brush and ink) painter seeks not only to reveal as much beauty as possible but also to hide as much as possible. The suggestiveness, the blank spaces, the thin traces of a delicate brush line all portray the inexhaustible mystery of the truly beautiful. A Japanese gardener constructing a rock and stone Zen garden will often hide the massive part of a particular rock under the raked sand so that one must imagine from the shape and configurations on top what the rest must be like. In Japanese flower arrangement, there is a preference for the half-opened bud. Latent, hidden, mysterious powers are present in these artworks.

Art inspires us to look at ourselves. A painting, a statue, a garden, a flower arrangement urge us to search in ourselves for the qualities of mystery, potential, perception, many-sidedness, incompleteness. When one looks at a sparse orchid painting or the emptiness of a Zen garden, one can imagine that a good person can have such emptiness—leading to fullness. A person can have this combination of opposites. The importance of all the senses and the possibility of intuitive perception are placed before us by art. When St. Paul wrote about our spreading the fragrance of God everywhere because "we are the aroma of Christ" (2 Cor. 2:15), he was speaking, as if looking at flowers, of a virtue which already exists in us—a virtue which is present in the midst of our transgression and partial knowledge and emptiness.

Art reminds us of the possibility of a full human life. Full—in the sense of the exercise of our imagination, the use of our perceptions and senses, the interacting forces of yin and yang, the acceptance of the unknown and the incomplete. The full human life is known in its absences, its blankness, its mysteriousness, its "dark nights of the soul." Artwork reminds us of the gaps in ourselves and in the world. C. G. Jung spoke of the "shadow side" of our lives. The dark side of the moon is always there in our personal cosmos. The unknowability of God, the Tao, the Buddha are brought home to us by art. Our yearning to be closer to such first principles and powers and yet our separation from them are aspects of the power of art. As Robert Grant's words to the hymn tune "Lyons" put it, based on Psalm 104, "His chariots of wrath the deep thunderclouds form; and dark is his path on the wings of the storm." Art reminds of the things about God which for us—like Job—are removed and mysterious, as well those things which we can only see "in a mirror dimly" (1 Cor. 13:12).

1. Describe any painting, sculpture, or architectural design that has placed you in a yin mode in understanding it—acceptance, "letting go," responsiveness, immediacy, directness.

2. Describe a piece of art that has helped you, in any way, to overcome the busy rush of your life. To "be still and know that I am God."

3. Can you accept the "unknowableness" of God? As you think about faith, is this unknowableness discouraging or affirming? What art form portrays this unknowableness best for you?

FIVE

WORSHIP AND PRAYER

Great Buddha sits, while
cherry blossoms blow,
Filling his lap of bronze
with faint pink snow.
      Kikaku

One thing I have asked of God,
that I will seek after;
to live in the house of
God all the days of my life,
to behold the beauty of God,
and to inquire in God's temple.
      Psalm 27:4

HELP FROM EASTERN ORTHODOXY

In the age of the Reformation, a small group of Christians embarked on a spiritual experiment without using creedal statements to proclaim truth, liturgies or rites to symbolize goodness, or holy images or icons to reflect beauty. They are known as the Society of Friends, or Quakers, called to be a sign of the age of the spirit by disengagement from the visual arts.

Much earlier in history a larger group of Christians had embarked on a spiritual experiment with the aid of creeds, liturgies, and holy images as revelations of truth, goodness, and beauty. They are known as the Orthodox church, called to be a sign of the age of the spirit by engaging the visual arts.

In the present day of fatigue and malaise among Western Christians, Pentecostal and charismatic movements attempt to bring spiritual renewal, but, typically, they ignore the visual arts, choosing the Quaker option—silence in worship, spiritual dedication in social service, and closeness in community—over the Orthodox. Perhaps there is a reason today, we believe, to lean toward the Orthodox rather than the Quaker as a redirection of our spiritual lives.

The Protestant theologian Paul Tillich once spoke of the Quaker truth and the Quaker mistake. The Quaker truth, he explained, is that everything, seen through the eyes of faith, is sacramental—an insightful and powerful concept. Nothing exists that does not reflect and communicate the power and glory of God. But, he contended, if we do not have established sacraments whose purpose it is to make us aware of life's sacredness, we might never perceive that all life is sacred. This may be the Quaker mistake. Mircea Eliade and others call attention to set-apart liturgical places and times as being essential in a person's or a group's religious experience—something very different from our homogenous lives, a "break in plane."

Anthony Ugolnik, a professor of English at Franklin and Marshall College, wrote in *The Illuminating Icon,* that the Eastern church, especially its sense of beauty and concern for the visual arts, might inform and enrich both the foundation and the expression of Christian faith and life in the West today. Both of the present authors have come from a tradition deeply embedded in Reformation theology, particularly English and American Puritanism, but we find that the Eastern church casts new illumination on questions of faith and spiritual life. We have also learned much from the Buddhism and the Taoism of China and Japan, especially the practice in these traditions of meditatively looking at a landscape painting or sitting contemplatively beside a Zen garden.

61

Ugolnik explains the complex aesthetic that undergirds Russian faith and culture by comparing it with our own. In the West, beauty has an indistinct and diversionary character and is subordinate to the truth, especially scientific truth, which is conceived of as always supreme. In the West, beauty typically appears as temptation, a force that can distract. Further, in the West we appropriate the beautiful in a privatistic manner, as an expression of individual taste.

In Eastern Christianity, beauty has a superior character and dominates; it is distributive rather than appropriative. It is never a matter of individual preference, for it has an existence grounded in social reality and is expressive of social perceptions of goodness and truth. In the East, the question of aesthetics is at the very heart of the church's concern for truth and goodness.

In the United States both the church and the academy tend to ignore the issue of aesthetics because we have made it fundamentally a matter of personal taste, placing beauty solely in the eyes of the beholder. Of course, we have done the same with goodness and truth, both of which have been relativized and privatized. Beauty is, in our culture, a neutral religious category and therefore auxiliary to our worship.

We, in the West, have been so estranged from the East and so prejudiced about Christianity in the East that we have lost our ability to perceive its significance for us. All that we see in Orthodox liturgy is elaborate vestments, icons, and a host of visual stimuli that to our word-centered Puritan consciousness is decadent and in our masculine culture effeminate. We cannot understand how, in the face of poverty, money can be spent on the visual arts as necessary for worship.

Nevertheless, beauty in the liturgy is central to an Orthodox understanding of worship because its function is to attract us to and envelop us in the good and the true. Beauty and the visual arts are judged not by personal gratification but by communal criteria of truth and goodness. The visual is intended to reveal God, who is both incarnate and hidden, whose reign has both come and is yet to come. The issue for the Orthodox is seeing clearly, imaging correctly, perceiving accurately.

The image of the saint is not venerated—the faith of the saint is. The saints are models of those who see goodness, truth, and beauty clearly. Images of the saints are to reveal to us a spiritual salvific beauty that is the criterion for life in Christ, life in the church. They are to reveal to us how our lives can be penetrated by the divine and manifest the divine.

As an Orthodox teacher of one of us once said, "I can feel [intuit] a sense of God's presence when I am with this or another icon. This saint is a spiritual woman. She is the most beautiful person I know." Georges Florovski once commented that beauty binds together those who submit collectively to its attraction. It binds the object and our perception of the object. It will not succumb easily to rational analysis.

Today there is a new wave of evangelistic emphasis on the text and oral witness which seems to go along with simplicity and starkness in architecture—but something is lacking. We need an alternative vision of life in tension with the world. We need to be placed for a time with all the saints in God's reign. We need a vision so that we can be aware of the gap between it and our reality. We need an experience of resurrection in a fallen world.

The act of understanding in the West has tended to be bound within the context of the book. In the Western encounter with the word of God, Christians relate to a verbal text. The question is how to wrestle meaning from the book. Truth comes through the book. The word of God comes to us bound between the covers of the Bible. God's word is considered embodied within a text, a powerful and historic concept. What is important to acknowledge, however, is that this conviction is cultural, that is, it is learned. Alternatives are possible and may be essential to Christian faith and life.

In the Eastern church it is different. While we say, "Take up and read," they will say, "Look up and see." In the West the Enlightenment, which corresponds with the Protestant Reformation, makes reading and hearing more important, especially for Protestants, than seeing. The Christian East and West approach Christian imagery and visual arts differently. They both use images, but they think differently about the images they produce.

East and West also differ in the way they use imagination, a difference whose roots go back to the dispute over the role of images in worship. The East invested art and the world of the imagination with sacramentality. In the West art might have a didactic, illustrative function, but the encounter with God was through the word. Reading, not imaging, is the central metaphor for discerning meaning.

Throughout the history of the church, iconic and iconoclastic positions have had their advocates, and each has defended its position theologically. God became human and is an incarnate God of history who can be imaged. Truth is revealed in the sacraments, which are outward and visible signs of inward and spiritual reality,

63

producing the art and life of worship. The Word is seen in bread and wine. Or, from the iconoclastic perspective, God is an invisible, unchangeable, eternal God who cannot be captured by the imagination. Truth is revealed in the words of Scripture, the science of theology. The Word is heard in the act of preaching.

From the outset the great tradition of the Eastern church through its iconic art directs us toward a perception of beauty based on the Gospels which is an expression and experience of holiness, focusing on the transfiguration of Christ and through Christ the transfiguration of the whole of creation. Perfect beauty is the beauty of God's face in the human, the icon of the crucified risen Jesus. The glory of the resurrection shines from a face which achieved the highest perfection or beauty through suffering on a cross. As St. Cyril reminds us, the temporal dimension of the incarnation and passion forms the beauty of the Son of God.

Whereas in the West, orthodoxy was understood as right speaking, in the East it was understood as right imagining, which explains why, in the East, the church has established rules for both the content and style of a sacred picture or icon. Protestants have no such rules. With a passion for the secular, Protestants contend that it is not necessary to go to holy places for inspiration, to worship in holy space, or to be in the presence of holy art to experience God. God can be experienced anywhere and everywhere. The most radical of Protestants deprecate the sacraments. Moreover, insofar as Protestantism also carries within itself an element of protest against all tradition, it tends toward the iconoclastic. Protestants continue to place the auditory over the visual, the Word heard over the Word envisioned, and have done so for so long that many do not even recognize the loss or the cost. The loss can be seen as a secularized world without God's presence and action, a new humanism that affirms belief in God but acts as if everything is up to us.

SEEING DIRECTLY

In her book *Image and Insight,* a significant innovative study of visual understandings in Western Christianity and secular culture, Margaret Miles contends that the historiography of Western Christianity is inadequate in that it deals primarily, if not solely, with verbal texts. After an immense struggle over the legitimacy of making and then venerating images in the late Patristic period, the Christian church came to see in the visual arts tremendous theological possibilities. An early ecumenical council recognized that art has a sacramental power.

The emphasis changed, however. Miles reminds us that religion has repeatedly been described as a way of seeing—seeing not merely in the actual sense, but in the metaphorical sense, perception leading to and becoming faith. Religion uses eyesight to point to insight, urging a seeing through and beyond the existential surface of life that enables the essential nature of reality to be revealed and experienced. The Puritans were mistrustful of the visual arts, perhaps, because they knew they were a powerful medium, but open to misunderstanding and confusion. They preferred the verbal arts because they appeared more manageable, secure, and sure.

Right thinking and doctrine have had a tendency to make reason both the source of religious knowledge and its judge. While some theologians have asserted the importance of the religious affections, and people have often become excessively concerned with pietistic feelings, church educators have been more concerned with teaching doctrine than encouraging religious experience. It is good to remember that throughout the Middle Ages and much of the Renaissance, Western art was explicitly Christian. However, the Enlightenment combined with the Reformation estranged the church and the arts. The artists sought liberation from the restraint of the church, and the church turned its back on the artists. By the eighteenth century the divorce was all but complete. While we have never been without examples of great religious art, they have typically been restricted to galleries and museums. With a few outstanding exceptions church architecture is unimaginative or simply reproduces space from another historical period and/or culture. While business and industry have become the patrons of the visual arts, few great paintings or sculpture adorn churches.

65

The engagement of vision in worship was experientially validated for medieval people by its fruits in love and piety. Vision was understood as the most appropriate access to God. The sight of the consecrated host had a salvific effect equal or superior to ingesting it. Vision was considered a fully satisfactory manner of communion and communication.

During the period which followed, Protestants and Roman Catholics condemned the church's dependence on the visual. Both recognized the verbal and auditory aspects of religious life. However, Protestants did more than attempt to reform an overdependence on the visual—they denied its validity. As Luther boldly established, "The ears are the only organ of a Christian." The result was a language-oriented religion and culture in which the only remaining art form was music.

Nevertheless, as Miles points out, the historic association of artistic images and religion was not an accident. Religion requires images. Until the sixteenth century, art and religion were interwoven; then the voices of reform shouted down the visual and proclaimed the importance of religious language. The results were disastrous. Systematic theology as we know it began in the eighteenth century, the Age of Reason, in which we enshrined truth in propositional form without recognizing the limits of an enterprise in which the supernatural is defined in rational terms.

Theologians have been hard on art. Barth, while admiring the crucifixion painting by Grünewald, declared that images and symbols have no place at all in a building chosen for Protestant worship. Gordon Kaufman writes a book entitled *Theological Imagination* but contends that only verbal discourse belongs to theology. Too often we have permitted a wedge to be driven between subjective experience and objective reflections, between the intuition and the intellect, between the sacred and the profane, between revelation and theology.

The French philosopher Gabriel Marcel describes the infinite possibilities of grace as being like scattered pollen on the summer air. But there can be no fertilization until the pollen reaches a flower that is ready and able to receive it. There can be no revelation until the message of the Gospel reaches those with the eyes to see and the ears to hear—and it cannot do this until it is given living expression, not once and for all, but over and over in each generation.

It should be as natural for Christians as it is for those in the vivid Hindu tradition to have a positive relationship to the visual arts, for Christians believe in the incarnation of the divine in human form, which implies an acceptance of the rest of creation as embodying that very same creative energy. One of the major divergences of the early church was the view of the Manichaeans that spirit alone was good and that matter was evil or indifferent. It is the function of the artist to renew the tradition that matter is good. John Berger in *Permanent Red* emphasizes that iconic art reveals that the incarnation really took place in matter. In Christ, matter became spiritual, impregnated with the nonmaterial, the holy, the Spirit of God.

Aiden Nichols, a Dominican priest from Scotland, wrote *The Art of God Incarnate,* a seminal work on the theology of visual symbol, challenging us to discover in the visual arts a mode that goes beyond the limitation of words in modern theology. He makes the point that we now live in a highly visual epoch of history. The power of visual images, mediated by television in particular, has become a major factor in the shaping of the modern mind. The importance of art is that it initiates us, through its own aesthetic structure, into a new world of meaning.

We must never forget that the Word of God refers to both deed and speech acts. As Christians we are called to proclaim God's good news in both word and example. Liturgical rites include both rituals and prescribed words as well as ceremonials and prescribed actions: When we limit ourselves to the words of Scripture, worship becomes preaching and Christian life talking.

In a typical Protestant liturgy there is little to see but much to hear. Words not images dominate. Is it any wonder children feel left out and bored? To pray we close our eyes. To gaze upon the consecrated bread is considered strange at best. Complaints go like this: "I cannot hear." Few of us in the Western church understand how deeply the visual arts affect the perception of meaning. What we see—candles, icons, light and shadows, vestments, spaces—are more important than we admit. Augustine said, concerning the consecrated bread, "Be what you see, receive who you already are"—which is difficult to do if you are not looking.

Consider the baptismal bowl, which is stored in a corner and brought out only on special occasions. Exotic flowers from a florist shop or fake flowers are often more dominant than any authentic Christian symbol. Typically, congregants gaze upon a choir dressed in elaborate robes instead of images of the saints. How many can say, "I can see and sense the presence of God in this space"?

While church architecture is intended to serve a function, that is, to provide a space for worship, it does much more. It both manifests and structures our perception of reality. We shape our space and then in turn our space shapes us. If our understanding of God is dominated by an emphasis on God's transcendence, we seek sacred emptiness; the beauty of holiness is the beauty of the mysterious void. But our emphasis is also on God's immanence, and we seek sacred presence; the beauty of holiness is the beauty of the mysterious manifested. We often overlook the second point, namely, that an incarnational view of God and therefore of goodness and truth requires beauty and visual representation.

Liturgical art, art in whose presence we pray, makes visible the unseen presence of God so we can relate and perceive. We must never confuse such art with what it reveals. Idolatry is always an issue, but the worship of the Bible and the treating of preaching as an end in itself is also a form of idolatry.

When the pulpit is the focal point, the preacher becomes a performer. People attend church to listen to the sermon, and hearing the sermon becomes worship. The architecture is focused on hearing. The only remaining art form is music, and often it too becomes performance; listening to the organ and the choir become more important than joining in the singing of hymns.

There is a painting in Santiago, Chile, *The Lord of Patience*, in which Jesus is sitting down with deep wounds, clots of blood, sad, defeated eyes, his head resting in his hands. How different from the peaceful eyes of the triumphant risen Christ, the *Pantocrator* of a Byzantine mosaic. The first is the Christ of the oppressed, the second the Christ of the strong. Which is the Christ we see? There are both reminder and hope here. Should not we who rule gaze on the prophetic, lacerated Christ and those who are oppressed gaze on the liberating Christ?

If our liturgy is to be effective in making Christians we will need to place greater attention on the visual image we present, whether through architecture, art, vestments, or symbolic actions. What we see is what we become. We shape what we see and then what we see shapes us.

"TEACH US TO PRAY"

How do the visual and the lessons that Eastern Orthodoxy has placed before us help in prayer life? Perhaps there is one common ingredient running through all forms of prayer—a desire to be connected and in communion with God's Spirit. Whether we intercede, petition, confess, or adore, we are attempting to search for God's providence and care. In our prayers, one way or another, we try in faith to accept and live in the great blessing of Moses to the children of Israel just before his death: "The eternal God is a dwelling place, from underneath the everlasting arms" (Deut. 33:27). In our prayers we try to become like Job, who found, at the end of his ordeal, that the realm and power of God's providence could be compared to the stars in the heaven, the expanse of the sea and "the skirts of the earth" (Job 38:13).

So often we close our eyes when we pray. It does shut out the world and, perhaps, helps us to concentrate and move into another place. But the spirit and the power of prayer can be found with our eyes open as we search for this connection and communion with divine energy. We do not need to follow for all of our lives the advice often given to children: "Close your eyes and say your prayers." Sometimes when we pray with our eyes closed our consciousness narrows and we become trapped. In Mahayana Buddhism, meditation is done with the eyes open, at least partly so, so that one may be conscious always of one's particular place at the moment, the presence of shadow and light, the sense of being connected with *ch'i*, energy, outside one's self.

Seeing deeply into an object of art or being acutely conscious of the dimension and configuration of a religious space can be an act of prayer. One of us as a young teenager was taken during a spring vacation to Washington, D.C. The memory of that trip which abides is not that of cherry blossoms and baseball playing in the park with father and brothers, but the overwhelming experience of walking up the steps at the Lincoln Memorial, entering, and gazing at the statue of the Great Emancipator. There was hiding behind a column when parents came to say it was time to leave. There in the Rotunda and in the presence of the seated, brooding

69

figure came a feeling of awe, a dimly grasped vision of freedom, an unformed sense of gratitude and thankfulness, and a rough sense of a nation's history. Eyes open produced a vivid awareness of a host of meanings.

Even more so, perhaps, is such a visual experience powerful in the space of a church. The work of Tadao Ando, a Japanese architect who designs and builds both secular and sacred spaces, is an example. To be present in his Church of the Light in Osaka, Japan, with eyes open is to make a connection with God's sustaining Spirit. One sits in a stark, boxlike concrete room. In the wall over the altar are two slits in the form of a cross to admit light from the outside. The possibility of direct communion with God without distraction is powerfully present in the space. The light shining through the cross from the outside into one's space suggests readiness to hear and to answer. When the eye roams meditatively over the gray-white, natural color of the walls, a sense of the divine Spirit is immediate and present. Such seeing becomes a deep, prayerful act of recognition and thanksgiving.

In Saint Mary's Episcopal Church in West Jefferson, North Carolina, Ben Long IV has painted a fresco entitled *The Mystery of Faith*. Long depicts in the foreground the crucified Christ, hanging on a cross which is rudely held in the dirt by rough stakes at the foot; in back, somewhat indistinct, is the figure of the risen Christ, simply clothed, arms outstretched in a welcoming gesture. To gaze on this modern fresco becomes a prayer, adding faith-centered details to the meaning of communion and connection. To see the fresco in open-eyed prayer is to grasp the sense that God is connected with us in suffering and death, but also in exaltation and new life. To see the fresco and to spend time in its presence is to grasp without words the specific Christian communion God offers us. While seeing, one may offer prayers of petition and adoration—or one may just be there without words in another form of prayer.

Eyes open, concentration, seeing into—these are so important in a prayerful communion with God. In the meditative tradition of Zen Buddhism, one is often urged before *zazen,* meditation, to fix one's gaze on a painting depicting the nature of the Buddha or of the *dharma,* law or reality. One such painting, by Ma Lin, a medieval Chinese Buddhist scholar, is called simply *Sunset* (see plate

13). The painting shows a valley, indistinctly bounded by mountains or hills, with a few birds flying across. The impression that emerges upon seeing this painting for a length of time is emptiness and blankness. The painting relates to the Buddha himself, who pushed aside attachments, contradictions, and desires in order to be empty and fresh for a different life. Implicit in responses to the painting is an acceptance of the place of silence in this tradition. A line of poetry often is placed beside the painting: "A bird cries out and the mountains become yet more silent." In the New England Congregational church where one of us grew up, there is a stained-glass window picturing Jesus at the door of a simple dwelling, lantern in one hand, other hand raised to knock: "Listen, I am standing at the door, knocking; if you hear my voice and open the door, I will come into you and eat with you, and you with me" (Rev. 3:20). To look at this window, with either darkness or light behind, becomes the beginning of a petition to let Christ come into one's life.

Barry Lopez, an environmental writer and storyteller, writes about the power of imagination in seeing: "What one imagines in the new landscape consists of conjecture, for example, about what might lie beyond that near horizon of small hills. . . . At a deeper level, however, imagination represents the desire to find what is unknown, unique, or far-fetched—a snowy owl sitting motionless on the hips of a musk ox, a flower of a favorite color never before reported, tundra swans swimming in a winter polynya."[1] Seeing does stimulate our imagination—and moves our prayerful response and petitions to a larger realm. In seeing a fresco of the crucifixion we can imagine ourselves in need and in guilt at the foot of the cross; in seeing the representation of an empty valley we can sense the need for silence before the majesty of God; in seeing the painting of Jesus outside a door we, who are inside, may ask that we have the will to lift the latch.

In Zen Buddhism, there is a form of meditation known as *basho zazen*, place meditation. After attempting to quiet one's self and center one's self, one imagines one's self in a special and favorite place. Imagination is given its run; one moves in the energy of the chosen place to reflect on its meaning and its claim upon the meditator; one also asks, compassionately, about the needs of such a

71

place. Prayer through seeing and imagining becomes an ever-expanding form of energy and revelation in our spiritual lives.

When one of his disciples said to him, "Lord, teach us to pray," Jesus did teach the best known words in Christian liturgy, "Our Father, who art in heaven . . ." But he also taught his disciples in their petitions for understanding and their expressions of gratitude to see the fig tree, the sower, the sea of Galilee, the mustard seed, the lost sheep—to behold the beauty of Christ in the temple where he spoke his first public words. He calls us to do the same, to use our eyes and our imagination to express our thanksgiving in prayer and to discover what we truly seek.

FOR REFLECTION AND DISCUSSION

1. In the Eastern Orthodox church, both Russian and Greek, there is much to see—vestments, icons, a walkway around the church, incense pots, paintings. Do these add to worship? Do you wish your church used more visual aids befitting your tradition?

2. Many say the silence and the plainness of a Quaker worship service have a special beauty. How would you describe such beauty?

3. In praying is it helpful to "go" to a special place—and "see" it and be in it while praying?

SIX

LEARNING AND GROWTH

Finally, beloved, whatever is true, whatever is honor-
able, whatever is just, whatever is pure, whatever is
pleasing, whatever is commendable, if there is any excel-
lence . . . think about these things.

Philippians 4:8

You and I are just swinging doors. This kind of under-
standing is necessary. This should not even be called
understanding; it is actually the true experience of life
through Zen practice. . . . Each one of us is in the midst
of myriads of worlds.

Shunryu Suzuki, Zen Mind, Beginner's Mind

WAYS OF LEARNING

In his book *The Man Who Mistook His Wife for a Hat,* Oliver Sacks offers case studies of persons who are accomplished artists but who are dismissed by society because they appear to be dysfunctional. There is Madeleine J., a sixty-year-old, congenitally blind woman with cerebral palsy who had been babied since birth. Although she learned to read Braille, she never left home and never was encouraged to use her deformed, spastic hands. Admitted to St. Benedict's Hospital near New York City and encouraged to use her hands for the first time, she began to recognize objects for the first time in her life. Having asked for clay, she began to make models reminiscent of the sculpture of Henry Moore. Within a year she was known as the blind sculptress of St. Benedict's. Her artistic ability appeared miraculous. Who could have dreamed that within this congenitally blind, aged, inactivated, overprotected woman lay the germ of an astonishing ability to communicate through art, as well as an artis-tic sensibility that could germinate and blossom after remaining dormant for sixty years?

Another case concerns twenty-one-year-old José, a young man who was mentally retarded and autistic and who suffered from violent seizures. With some encouragement, he began to draw and revealed a gift for the specific and the concrete. Soon he manifested the talents of a "naturalist," an artist who could draw literally and in great detail. Because of our prejudices, persons like José never have the opportunity to accompany scientific expeditions and make drawings of rare species, or illustrate textbooks, nursery tales, and biblical stories, or create artistic masterpieces in stained glass or mosaic.[1] Today we institutionalize such persons and by so doing not only oppress them, but deny ourselves their gifts.

We too easily speak of "the disabled"; putting it more properly, all of us are abled differently. Regretfully, our culture values one form of ableness over others, thereby not only refusing to recognize other abilities but labeling them disabilities. Without those who are abled differently than we are, we are all diminished.

When we use our artistic judgment and abilities, so often hidden, we learn about ourselves and frequently discover a power of knowledge. One of us has been teaching a course on East Asian religions which involves dealing with major texts such as the *Tao Te Ching* (The Book about the Way and Its Power), the *I Ching* (The Book of Changes), the Buddhist *Diamond Sutra* and the *Heart Sutra*. Probably the most difficult to teach is the *I Ching* because of its long history of interpretation, its mysticism, and its connection with prediction—that is, its offering of approaches to problems through the use of hexagrams consisting of solid yang lines and broken yin lines, as well as through the study of accompanying prose and poetry.

One approaches the *I Ching* by asking it a question in a ritual setting. Students volunteered to participate in the ritual, which was performed in a traditional ceremony, using incense, wearing robes, and casting *yaro* sticks to construct hexagrams, with the questioner sitting in yang position facing south, the caster in yin position facing north. A student asked this question: "How can I ease the burden placed on my mother by the death of my father?" Two hexagrams are produced by a ritualistic casting. The second or "concluding" hexagram which emerged was number two out of the possible sixty-four, known as *K'un,* the Receptive, six lines, all broken, all yin:

—— ——
—— ——
—— ——
—— ——
—— ——
—— ——

The hexagrams and the accompanying texts were discussed by the class and questions were put to the questioner and the caster. Illumination was cast on the problem by the text and the discussion. But the student questioner found that looking, meditatively, at the simple configuration of lines and "seeing" into the configuration's totally yin presentation gave him the most insight into his agonizing question. To be totally receptive, to be a listener, to be a receiver, to be open in the middle of himself in heart and mind, to be present to his mother without an agenda, to be yin—these were ways in which he could "ease the burden." He carried the hexagram around with him on paper and in his mind. He drew it over and over. This simple, Chinese line drawing, emerging out of a ritual process, produced a healing, offered a new way of response, and taught him something about himself.

75

Contemporary philosophers, some of whom call themselves postmodernists, and contemporary artists frequently employ a classic Latin expression to express the connection between image and word or between art and principle—*ut pictura theoria,* theory as picture. They would say that a theory, a principle, a *logos* known as an explanatory order, emerges from an image, or a picturing. Einstein frequently used imagery and imagination in working on the problems of relativity and the understanding of mass and energy. Stephen Hawking, the English physicist, confesses that he thinks in pictures, mental images of the universe, rather than mathematical equations. Many historians claim that the scientific progress of the Renaissance was related to the positive attention paid to spatial imaging in the period.

The role of spatial intelligence and experience is, in part, to break down the usual estrangement between the arts and the sciences. Production in many human activities is connected with a move from picturing to the "word," or the result. Einstein moved to theories from contemplating images, and Hawking comes to know the world through mental pictures. Perhaps it can be said that the idea emerges from the image in many areas of life.

One of us was leading a church study group on the idea of creation. Very few parishioners would speak about this complicated idea. Suddenly, and without discussion, paper and crayons were handed out to the group. Each person was asked to draw his or her idea of creation. The responses were many: Some drew a colorful sunrise; others a tree of life; another attempted to represent the vastness of the ocean upon which something was moving; yet another pictured a Japanese rock and stone garden in which openness, blankness, simplicity dominated. The paintings were then passed around in small groups. Conversation picked up! People were amazed at the different ideas. More important, members of the group said that their idea of creation was in some kind of an abyss until they started to draw. Not that there was agreement about the meaning of creation, but there was a confirmation that the imaging had helped to produce an idea or a conception.

Hsieh Ho, a medieval Chinese artist and philosopher, wrote about the "principles" of aesthetic theory, which relate to poetry and calligraphy as well as to painting. The first two principles he identified are "rhythmic vitality" and "bone structure." A painter could present the reality of a subject, say, a running horse, by capturing the smooth flowing of the gait and the structure of legs, neck, back, and head. The idea of a horse would emerge from this imaging of rhythm and structure. And one would truly see what a horse is in such a painting.

Sometimes the imaging is only suggestive. It is often said that Western architects use a "digital" scheme of design—a this balanced by a that, with a concentration on sequence. The result is, as many Japanese and nontraditional Western architects point out, a design in the form of a "printout." Japanese and postmodernist architects in this country use an "analog" scheme—an art form that is suggestive, free, reduced. For example, a tree with entwining, choking ivy will be used rather than a graceful, classical statue at the entrance to a museum to mark an exhibit of art connected with Greek tragedy. The best of imaging, leading to a theory or an idea, is often scanty, easily passed by. When the image is taken in, however, the power of the idea emerges with suddenness and connection.

We ought not to equate knowledge with what is definite, objective, verifiable, and conceptual—that is, with what we can control, take apart, and put together for our purposes. A painting is not an object for us only to look at and evaluate; it is a subject to engage and question us. While still being critical and comparative, we can allow the energy and substance of a work of art to engulf us. We can allow it to have its own being.

We have been taught that the split between the cognitive and the affective is a false split, but we have a hard time applying this insight to actual learning skills. We are still trapped in the scientific and objective. We have difficulty teaching and learning that there are other forms of knowing. Susanne Langer in *Philosophy in a New Key* wrote of our ordinary forms of knowing, but commented that we possess other ways which do not lend themselves to calculation and quantification—forms of knowing which are for ambiguities, vision, mystery, beauty, compassion, and "unspeakable things."

TEACHING AND CURRICULUM

Few parents, taxpayers, school boards, and educators are committed to making the visual arts central to the curriculum of the schools. Art teachers are among the last to be hired and the first fired when a school budget is cut. With the exception of schools for the arts, the study of the history and philosophy of art is typically an elective, the study of art as drawing, painting, and sculpture typically an extracurricular activity. The exceptions prove the point. In an elementary school, art is often put at the end of the week, Friday afternoon, or during the time of the day when children are most tired, rather than first thing in the morning when they are most alert. The message is simply that art is not important. In the curriculum of schools, the visual arts are rarely considered essential or foundational to learning. All too often, they are not even considered supportive to foundational learning. Among parents, coloring books and crayons are more popular than paint, clay, or other materials which might encourage more creative expressions. Few parents long for their children to become painters or sculptors. By the time children have completed elementary school, art has been pushed to the periphery of educational concerns.

Most adults say that they cannot paint, draw, or sculpt. Few academics would accept the suggestion that an important doorway into history is through the visual arts. Even fewer would accept the suggestion that learning in their field can be enhanced by the engagement of students in the visual arts. It is as if educators were convinced that aesthetics had little to do with learning.

This estrangement of the arts and learning has a long history. Interestingly, in the curriculum of Harvard College and the College of William and Mary, our nation's earliest institutions of higher learning, the word "art" is never mentioned. What art existed in our nation's foundational years was primarily for utilitarian and decorative purposes. With the exception of Thomas Jefferson, one looks in vain for quotations from the founding fathers on concern for the arts. Tocqueville commented in the nineteenth century that we are a nation that prefers the useful to the beautiful, a nation in which education is an instrument rather than an ultimate value.

Of course, our belief in mass education was not founded primarily upon a passion for the development of the mind but for its supposed political and economic benefits. Today we are worried about our place in the world of politics and economics. A corresponding concern for education has emerged, but it is education that is not whole and will not in the long run benefit us.

Advocates for the teaching of English, mathematics, and science are many; advocates for the teaching of the visual arts few. There may have been a remarkable expansion of art museums and galleries. The growth in the market for sculpture, paintings, reproductions, and architecture may indeed have grown. But the majority of our citizens have little interest in the visual arts. A typical question put to a school board is: What does a person or society have to gain from the visual arts that would justify their place and expense in the curriculum?

It is a loaded question, for it asks us to defend the extrinsic value of the visual arts when they have none. In terms of education, the visual arts have only an intrinsic value. It is not necessarily the piece of sculpture or the painting that has value; it is the creation of it and our experience of it that has value. A work of art helps us learn to be more conscious of the persons and environment about us, to image the particularity and peculiarity of what is typically hidden from view, to contemplate life and acquire new insights, to be engaged by all of life as subject.

In his book *To Know As We Are Known,* Parker Palmer explains that teaching and learning typically rely on factual observation and logical analysis, which often keep the world at arm's length. It is the kind of knowledge that eliminates mystery and tries to put us in charge of an object world. As a result, we teach facts, a body of knowledge, and a consequent set of skills or techniques. We teach a static mode of relationships between the knower and the known, a way of being in the world which focuses on the outside of an object, a person, nature, history. Seldom are we taught to go inside in order to grasp the mysteries of nature or the psychology of a people and a culture behind historical data. But, says Palmer, this object-world approach by which we take apart and analyze so that we can understand, control, and put back together for our purposes is worse than unproductive. He argues that it is connected with the biblical notion of sin.

In the biblical myth of Adam and Eve we have an account of the first sin, which is interestingly an epistemological distortion. Adam and Eve were driven from the garden, a place of harmony and communion, not because they sought knowledge, but because they sought a particular kind of knowledge. They sought knowledge that excluded God and mystery, awe and wonder. They sought objective knowledge that would put them in charge and in control—powers and a role belonging to God alone. Or, as Palmer puts it, "In their [Adam and Eve's] refusal to know as they were known, they reached for a kind of truth that always leads to death."[2]

Knowing requires an open, personal relationship between the knower and the known. It implies a learning that interacts with the world, envisions the world as subject, and engages us. This is the attitude an artist brings to the world and that we can bring to an artistic creation. Aesthetic learning includes abilities to produce art, appreciate art, and reflect upon our experience of art.

Regretfully, art educators still argue over the merits of the studio approach of creating art versus the academic approach of studying art. Perhaps, even in a less than ideal world, the two can coexist. One of us taught for a number of years a course entitled "The Japanese Religious Aesthetic." Readings were done on general aesthetic theory; quizzes were given on terms associated with Japanese art forms, such as *shodo* (calligraphy), *cha-no-yu* (tea ceremony), *sumi-e* (brush and ink drawing); a final paper was written. But the heart of the course was a "diary project," in which students were to engage in one of the art forms studied while keeping a journal and to present their art to the class for explanation and discussion. At the beginning, some students were reluctant: "I can't draw with a pencil, let alone with a brush"; "Japanese *kanji* [characters] are beyond me"; "My legs won't let me sit that long to do the Japanese tea ceremony." Yet, as art projects were looked at, journals were shared, tea utensils were examined and tea was served, it became clear that the diary project was the most rewarding and instructive part of the course. The simplicity, directness, and openness of Japanese aesthetics were understood, if only in part—entered into by those students who had no previous acquaintance with these art forms and thought they had no ability to do them. Genuine learning took place.

We are more apt to acknowledge the role and vocation of the professional artist than we are to acknowledge the artist in each of us. Aesthetic expression is a way of keeping us human by reminding us that we are created in God's image, that we, too, have the capacity to be creative. By exercising that capacity, our learning takes us to deeper levels of meaning in any process of education.

Children naturally appreciate art, for there is a relationship between participating in art and appreciating art. As Madeleine L'Engle in her book *Walking on Water* writes, "All children are artists and it is an indictment of our culture that so many of them lose their creativity and their unfettered imaginations as they grow older."[3]

A child's vision is global: It takes in the undifferentiated whole and does not abstract details. This gives young children the freedom to distort color and shape imaginatively. Adults may see their art as unrealistic, but to children it is quite realistic. This syncretistic vision of children is never entirely destroyed and later becomes important in the art of adults. Indeed, if we can reunite this former syncretistic vision with a later analytic awareness we have a mature artist.

The great tragedy is what we do with young children and art, much of which works against their learning and desire at an early age to use their creative ability. Once again, we give them coloring books and encourage arts and craft activities, rather than encouraging more imaginative pursuits. A child begins with the mind and heart of the artist (see plate 14). But somewhere between the ages twelve and sixteen creative artistic ability begins to decrease and, unless nourished, will eventually atrophy.

Our human imagination is fragile. Our creative ability is easily lost. One of us remembers when a daughter was in preschool. We had set up the family room with an easel for painting, a table for clay molding, finger painting, and the like. On one wall we put a "painting of the month," a reproduction by a well-known artist, each month in a different style—abstract, impressionistic, realist. On the other wall was some of our family art including that of our daughter. One day Jill came home and said, "Daddy, draw me a table." The response was, "Oh Jill, you can draw a table." She burst into tears. "What's wrong?" I asked. "The teacher showed me how to draw a table and I can't do it." "Well, then, let me help you learn." We blindfolded each other and approached the table. We crawled up one leg, smelled, tasted, touched, rubbed the table. Then I said, "What color do you feel about this table? Use that color. What do you remember best about the table? Make it big. Add anything else that you remember." I did the same. Then I put up a series of "table paintings": our two tables, a cubist painting of a table, and an idealist painting of a table. "There are four beautiful tables. Each is of value and each helps us to understand tables better." Jill felt better.

81

As Charles Mountford writes in *The Artist and His Art in Australian Aboriginal Society,* there is no special artist class in an aboriginal society; every member, young and old, will sometimes be an artist. Not restricted to an elite, the "artist within" is a natural capacity of every human being, though some may have greater potential and, of course, if they are aided to develop that capacity, greater ability. If art becomes the terrain of the specialist, it is because the culture has made it so.

Howard Gardner in *Arts and Human Development* comments that while our culture requires the development of formal operations of the mind, which is a level of cognitive development, the artist does not. The artist need not deal with creation in propositional or hypothetical form. Formal operations may even at times serve to hinder artistic development, since the tendency to focus on underlying content, to abstract out meaning, to be explicit, systematic, and exhaustive in translating problems, to turn questions into logical propositions—all these may militate against the sensitivity necessary for the artist.

The stress on critical thought in adolescence is a mixed blessing. In primitive societies all members are artists because they are not impaired by knowledge of formal operations. During these middle years, the disciplines and techniques of art need to be taught along with an introduction to art history in order to help keep the imagination alive.

Maria Harris in the opening chapter of her seminal book *Teaching and Religious Imagination* recounts the following story. Miroslov Holub in his poem "Brief Thoughts on Maps" describes a Hungarian officer who sends a detachment of men into the Alps. There they encounter a blizzard and for days are assumed to be lost. Just when everyone at the base is sure they have all died in the storm they return, explaining that one of them had found a map in his pocket and, after the snow ended, used it to find their way back. When the officer looks at the map he discovers it is a map of the Pyrenees, not the Alps. But because they imagined the power to return home, aided by the idea of a found map, because they imagined they had the capacity to survive, they made the impossible possible.

Maria Harris tells of Mary Tully, "the greatest educator I ever knew," and a simple exercise Tully had her students do with clay. Tully suggested they play with the clay and discover what it could do; then she asked them to blindfold themselves while she gave these instructions: "A form exists within the clay you are holding in your hands and you are to discover it. As you work with the clay let it work with you. Give yourself time to concentrate and you will encounter a form taking shape; you will be able to feel it, to sense it, to know it. When that happens you can take off the blindfold and work from there."[4] The molding of clay is a metaphor for illuminating the learning process—fashioning and refashioning of the "lump" that life offers, giving flesh to something, embodying, forming. Harris speaks of teaching as a work of the religious imagination, the incarnation of subject matter, the embodiment of subject matter. Teachers are artistic agents who arrange an environment in which persons might be engaged with subject matter.

Elliot Eisner in his book *Educational Imagination* discusses the explicit, implicit, and null curriculum, the third one referring to what is left out. Aesthetics has been left out. Most educators have focused attention on the cognitive aspects of human, moral, faith, and psychological development and view maturity cognitively. We have forgotten the importance of aesthetic development, or what Gardner calls full participation in the artistic process. We know a person as a being whose intelligence and maturity are marked by the ability to engage in advanced cognitive processes of logical analysis and in advanced vocabulary and literary skills. But these alone can distort the human being. The imaginative, artistic, and the aesthetic are foundational to human development, for they enlarge our vision and deepen our insights.

All learning depends on the ability to image, to picture both accurately and imaginatively. We can deceive ourselves if we do not image accurately the way things appear, but we also need to be able to perceive what is not visible—to vision, to see, to picture with the imagination. All learning and growth depend on the combination of these abilities.

83

To vision the good, the true, and the beautiful; to image reality as it is now and as it might be; to perceive the difference—these capabilities are needed for any human community. To make images of reality so it cannot be missed and to make images of a vision desired can help to make possible the closing of the gap between them. To learn to appreciate the visual arts is to learn new and different ways of knowing, essential for a truly human society.

FOR REFLECTION AND DISCUSSION

1. Draw a picture or representation of the resurrection. Do new insights or emphases come as you work on your "art form"?

2. Can you make a drawing or sketch of "openness"? Does the making of it, and the final result, lead you to think afresh about people in your life, about religious ideas, about things to do, about yourself?

3. How can we keep "doing art" as we grow older, assuming that art is a necessary activity in learning, growth, and life?

CONCLUSION

Implications of Aesthetics for the Church

Climbing the mountain path, I see far down
The paper kites above a castle town.

Taigi

They came to Jericho. As he and his disciples and a large
crowd were leaving Jericho, Bartimaeus son of Timaeus,
a blind beggar, was sitting by the roadside. When he
heard that it was Jesus of Nazareth, he began to shout
out and say, "Jesus, Son of David, have mercy on me!"
Many sternly ordered him to be quiet, but he cried out
even more loudly, "Son of David, have mercy on me!"
Jesus stood still and said, "Call him here." And they
called the blind man, saying to him, "Take heart; get
up, he is calling you." So throwing off his cloak, he
sprang up and came to Jesus. Then Jesus said to him,
"What do you want me to do for you?" The blind man
said to him, "My teacher, let me see again." Jesus said to
him, "Go; your faith has made you well." Immediately
he regained his sight and followed him on the way.

Mark 10:46-52

85

SEEING AND FAITH

On a rainy October Sunday, we two authors worshiped together at
the Chapel of the Cross in Chapel Hill, North Carolina. The New
Testament lesson of the day was the above account of Bartimaeus,
the blind beggar who received his sight in a miraculous act of Jesus.
After the service, we talked about what we had seen in the chapel as
the liturgy and the service unfolded. We had seen a procession and
a recession; we had seen the host elevated and served; we had seen
people passing the sign of peace; we had seen the cross and the art
forms at the front of the chapel. For us, one a Congregationalist

and the other an Episcopalian, these experiences of seeing, we agreed, had for that time together enlarged our faith and made it more vivid. We were put in mind of the meaning of a spiritual journey as we watched the procession; we thought of providence and God's caring as we watched the light and changing hues in the chapel; we saw genuineness and openness among people as they touched and embraced one another in the exchange of peace.

On an Easter Sunday, one of us attended a small Congregational church in northern New England while visiting children and grandchildren. The minister announced in simple, direct style that the worship service would focus on "getting the picture"—seeing into the meaning of crucifixion and resurrection. The service would be based on chapters 20 and 21 of John, the last two chapters of the Gospels, the theme of which might be said to be: "If I am lifted up, I will draw all people unto me." Instead of a sermon, a large painting was held up, done by a parishioner in a church art group. There was a silhouette of Jesus standing against an outline of a hill with his arms at his side, his hands open and raised slightly toward the congregation. The coloring was delicate, but, at the same time, startling: The hill and the figure of Jesus were in a circle, with blending pink and red toward the outside of the circle and white around the silhouetted Christ in the center. There were no words anywhere on the painting. We were asked to study the painting for a period of minutes to take in the picture of a crucified Savior on a hill and also of an ascended Savior who is calling all to become followers. The seeing was powerful, each of us going an individual way into crucifixion and resurrection as we looked at an art form made not by a famous artist, but by a person like us. The experience was similar to that of watching homespun Easter pageants in which a cross is carried, Roman soldiers pound nails, an empty tomb is portrayed, and a doubting Thomas places his hand in the side of the resurrected Lord. Special meanings through seeing occurred without words.

In the chapel of the School of Theology at Doshisha University in Kyoto, Japan, there hangs a large crown of thorns suspended from the ceiling, directly over the communion table. Behind the crown is a floor-to-ceiling mosaic of color and indistinct figures. The figure at the very top of the glass mosaic is Christ, standing with his arms outstretched with a block for his face—the whole design barely suggestive of Christ's human form. One's eye goes back and forth between the rough, stark reality of the crown of thorns and the mosaic of color and of joy. As one looks at the two artworks, one is reminded of the definiteness and sharpness of suffering, pain, and death; one is also reminded, looking further at the glass, of the brightness, the expansiveness, the mystery of Christ's mercy. One sees tragedy but one also sees embracing acceptance and resolution of tragedy behind.

Seeing and faith go together. This is true not only in a southern Episcopal church, a New England Congregational church, and in a Japanese university ecumenical chapel, but also in other places and traditions. For instance, Frederick Franck, a Dutch Roman Catholic artist, wrote *Zen and the Art of Seeing,* a book of original sketches and handwritten text. He covers topics such as seeing the true nature of the particular, using the small and the insignificant in sketching, seeing the extraordinary in the ordinary, seeing oneself in the midst of those things being portrayed, seeing oneself as quiet and absorbing—all of which are ways of seeing that lead the reader into the Zen way.

How can the church encourage the art of seeing so that the world of faith may be entered? And, conversely, how can we nurture the beginnings of faith so that we can see the better, thereby maturing and enlarging our faith? How difficult it is when our congregational lives seem overburdened with doctrines and prescriptions and rules. How can the light, space, simplicity, immediacy of a Chartres or a Ryoan-ji enter our lives? How can the sense of both presence and absence—essential ingredients in an understanding of aesthetics—be demonstrated and "seen" in our churches?

The task of seeing beauty in nature is difficult enough, given our urban society. One of us, on a trip, heard in the midst of the grandeur of plains and distant mountains a local saying: "God is real in Saskatchewan." But people who live in cities are often cut off from such views. To see the beautiful in our church services and to move beyond seeing to faith is even more difficult in the face of stultifying liturgy, sameness of events, and dullness of the spoken word. How do we use our imagination, the right side of our brain, the yin side of our being in our worshiping communities?

ENLIVENING OUR COMMON LIFE

In his discerning work *The Structures of Scientific Revolutions,* Thomas Kuhn discusses the historical processes by which science shifts from one foundational way of understanding reality to another. For a time a tradition flourishes, such as the Newtonian worldview. It manifests itself as a paradigm, a way of understanding that undergirds all the work of the then-known scientific world. Along the way, however, anomalies appear. Some scientists begin to see that the current paradigm is not fully satisfactory for answering all the questions put to it. Slowly a new paradigm emerges, usually after a variety of attempts are made to find a new way. Eventually the later paradigm takes over and becomes the new tradition. E. H. Gombrich in *Art and Illusion* examined the history of art and discovered a similar process. For a time a tradition in art and in art interpretation flourishes; a style for expressing and understanding life exists. But then it becomes inadequate for a particular developing culture, and new styles are experimented with until a different one emerges as acceptable. Another tradition forms. The history of science is a history of paradigm shifts and so is the history of art.

This is important for those of us in the church to know. Artworks and art interpretation have been shifting in response to many cultural and societal pressures. To use only medieval or Renaissance art as "seeing" examples for the faith may put the church seriously out of touch with the times. Certainly, the church should be aware of developments in art, sculpture, and architecture that reflect the uncertainty of the times, the sense of absence, meaninglessness, gaps in our understandings.

A new way of interpreting art is emerging, offering yet another paradigm. John Dillenberger writes, "A painting can no longer be about something; it must itself be the something. . . . [there is] no world to be painted, only a world to be made into a painting."[1] John W. Cook speaks about the necessity of a work of art "doing its own work." When the meaning of the art form itself is allowed to emerge freely, there may be the occasion of a living visual theology.[2] The purpose of art, in this new religious sense, is to put meaning into the world, but not *a* meaning—revering a piece of art but not ascribing a specific meaning to it. Art communicates in a unique fashion; it must be lived with and accepted in its multiple dimensions, for it has unlimited power to illumine our experience.

Matthew Fox in his book *Original Blessing* writes about a new paradigm emerging in theology which parallels the shift taking place in art. Formerly, coming out of Augustinian and Reformation thought, the classical concerns of the fall and redemption were central. Today, alongside this traditional emphasis, there is a concern for "creation-centered" theology. The former stresses original sin, the latter original blessing; the older speaks of obedience, the new emphasizes creativity and responsiveness; duty is predominant in the former, beauty in the latter; faith, for the older, is in belief and, for the new, in imagination.

Art intrinsically opens itself up and we should be able to receive its multiple meanings and hopeful force. Martin Heidegger suggests that we translate the Greek word *aléthia* as "unconcealment" rather than "truth." Friedrich von Schiller, in writing on aesthetics, uses the German word *Anschauung,* which implies that we should be able to trust our organs of sense and engage in forms of direct perception, some of them arising unconsciously. The word also stresses an intuitive, rather than an abstract and analytical, way of seeing. Certainly the analytical faculty will be used, but the "knowledge about" that it employs should be combined with the immediacy of a knowledge *of* a work of art.

William James stated that the best way to understand what something means is to see what difference it makes. Take an artwork or even an idea and let it work in the stream of experience to find out what it means. See what happens. Contemporary postmodern thinkers are arguing for a reasserted pragmatism. Live in the "texts"; get inside them and see what happens to you. When you try to understand a piece of art, you are always inside anyway, seeing what is happening to you—it's like being in a room. If we try things out in the realm of art and see what our experience is, we might be able to do more interesting things and be more interesting to people in our congregations.

Charles Moore, the American architect of museums and of public and private buildings, states that architecture is a "choreography of the familiar." Art should be true to the complexity of life.

89

Paintings, sculpture, and photography that might be studied in our church congregations should deal with those situations and insights which we can immediately identify. Photographs and sketches dealing with the homeless and with the rebuilding work of Habitat are forms that might well speak to us. Paintings and photographs of the glories of nature, reflecting a creation-centered theology, are productive of discussion and instruction.

Liang Kai's painting *Shakyamuni Descending the Mountain,* with its combination of simplicity and forcefulness, shows the everyday concern for returning to the world and assuming responsible, participatory lives (see plate 15). Shakyamuni, or Buddha, does not stay up on the mountain, lost in rapture and contemplation. The art form of other traditions, particularly that of Buddhism and Taoism, stresses this familiar everydayness. We should be ready for the messages and inspiration which such art presents to us in our Christian fellowships. While it is true that we may never be able to understand fully another religious perspective, it is also true that there is no religious perspective that we cannot understand at all. The study of the art form of other traditions can be image shattering, broadening our perceptions and breaking apart the standard, stereotypical interpretations we have of the world and of ourselves.

We have such profoundly helpful art in our own culture, of course. For example, on the subject of the miraculous, but ordinary, meaning of the nativity, consider Pieter Brueghel's painting *The Census at Bethlehem* (see plate 16). It shows a typical midwinter day in a Flemish town. A merchant and a buyer are haggling over price, a young man flirts with a maiden, children play, a crowd lines up to pay yearly taxes, a laborer struggles with an overloaded cart. Life goes on—but in the lower center is an unnoticed carpenter with a bag of tools leading a donkey on whose back rides a young woman.

Architecturally, the church has adapted styles from every historical period according to the circumstances of its people and their culture, as well as the needs of various rites developed over time. Thus, in the course of centuries, the church has brought into being a treasury of architectural art, a witness to faith—contributions which must be preserved. However, the art of our own day, coming from every race, region, and culture, needs to be given free scope and encouraged if we are to be faithful to God's presence in an ever-changing world.

It makes no sense to build a New England meeting house in Japan, or a Gothic cathedral in the twenty-first century. We need to be willing to transform our present buildings to speak to the present as well as to the past. Most church spaces can both maintain continuity with the past and still be altered to speak to the present. A Quaker meeting house, for example, is a form of art. Within its relationship of line, color, and space is housed historical meaning and the spirit of a tradition. Indeed, much contemporary church architecture is moving in the direction of the Friends' simplicity. Correspondingly, Quakers, redirecting their traditional emphasis, can provide space within their meeting houses for contemporary painting, sculpture, and crafts, using a variety that changes with the season, where persons and small groups can gather to meditate and pray.

What is important in our creating of church space is a general set of principles that can be applied to various cultures, times, and places. Church architecture requires a climate of hospitality, that is, a place where the stranger can feel welcome, where all the people, young and old, can feel comfortable with one another and share a sense of being at home as a spirit-filled family. Minimally this implies space that welcomes persons with disabilities, but in terms of worship space it implies a type of seating that suits the varied needs of different liturgies. Sometimes, though not always, chairs are better than pews. At any rate, seating that encourages participation and community is better than that which tends to make members of the congregation individual spectators.

At the same time, church architecture requires a climate in which mystery can be experienced. We need immanent space which invites personal contemplation and interiority, but also transcendent space which points beyond itself and the people present to the holy. Only the very best we humans can produce is worthy of God and is capable of bearing the weight of mystery and wonder in any particular culture or time in history. Nothing fake, cheap, shoddy, pretentious, superficial, or drawn haphazardly from other cultures or periods can do that. Historical imitations and prefab furnishings and decorations deny artists and artisans the opportunity to use their gifts, along with the finest material available, to create space for the church to make a statement in the present time and place.

For too long we have worried more about audibility than visibility. But what we see is as important as what we hear. Worshipful space makes possible and encourages our faith journeys. In our church space there are three spaces or objects of equal importance for Christians at worship, the lines and shapes of which change with culture and time: a simple but dignified pulpit or reading desk to emphasize the importance of hearing and reflecting upon the Scriptures; an altar table in the midst of the people, approachable for a common meal; and a baptistry capable of immersing or anointing infants and adults in the presence of the total community.

Simplicity and integrity are important so as not to detract from various objects and symbols present. Decorations, flowers, art, hangings, vestments, and the like need to be genuine, but not so elaborate as to draw attention to themselves. They are intended to create an environment for worship. The biggest difficulty, of course, is that people often become idolatrous about church architecture and objects, turning altars and pulpits into ends rather than means. What is important is to wed "a house of God," with its focus on symbolic space, with "a house for the people of God," with its focus on functional space—to bring both concepts into an imaginative whole. As we celebrate our faith, we must necessarily involve the whole person, all our human facilities: body, mind, the senses, the imagination, our emotions, reason, memory, and skill. We humans worship with all of our lifefulness, and no aspect can be ignored when creating the space in which we live as the people of God.

Aesthetic considerations reflect directly on our understanding and use of liturgy. As we become a more visual culture, children and later generations of adults will respond more fully to what they see than to what they hear. Or better, they will have difficulty hearing what they do not also see. The activity of the liturgy as a visual action, therefore, will become increasingly important, even as it was before the Reformation and the Enlightenment. Protestant churches which ignore this fact will probably become increasingly marginal. Liturgy in all traditions will need to be understood as a work of art comprised of visuals, drama, music, and dance involving the whole congregation in a living piece of art. Costumes and vestments worn and actions performed will become increasingly important, but caution is needed lest a gap be created between the clergy and lay people. For example, dressing lay people in vestments to read the Bible or pray the prayers of the people works against the ministry of the laity by creating "a clergy for a day." Similarly, having only clergy read the lessons or say the prayers works against the ministry of the whole church. The liturgy belongs to the people; the clergy preside and play an enabling role. It is essential that what we see the clergy do points to the priesthood of all believers. We must give thought to what people see being done by whom and when, for these liturgical actions shape our understanding of ourselves and of our life together in the church.

Iconography is seldom used in our Western churches. We need to look to Greek Orthodox and Russian Orthodox churches to discover the long, meaningful history of the use of icons. To use iconography is not to engage in idol worship. It is rather to use an icon—a painting, a statue, a medallion—as a visual way of pointing to the meaning of the faith. We also can learn from the meditative practices of Eastern religions where paintings, calligraphy, and designs are used to approach the meaning of emptiness, simplicity, Buddhahood. Icons worthy of such use are those which have the qualities of immediate recognition for practice—they have an everydayness and directness that stir the imagination.

93

Henri Nouwen wrote about a Pentecost icon, depicting Acts 2, which allows the viewer to enter into the ordinariness of a gathering of people, the questions and challenges and doubts held by those gathered, the promises and call of the Holy Spirit. Ryokan, the Zen painter, poet, and "comic spirit," drew the two pieces of calligraphy for "heaven" and "earth" together in one flowing motion (see plate 17). One need not know the strokes of these two pieces of calligraphy (in fact, they are so stylized that many Japanese and Chinese would not recognize the configuration of the brush strokes). But one can catch the gist of this amazingly simple rendition, namely, that heaven and earth belong together, that there is no "above" and "below"—heaven is now and now can be heaven—which is emphasized by a dot.

An individual or a small group might look intently at the Pentecost icon or Ryokan's *Heaven and Earth* and see what happens. The contemplative practice of looking at and inquiring about the meaning of an icon is not a sign of withdrawal or retreat. Like *zazen* in Zen Buddhism, the practice puts one in mind of crucial matters in a religious perspective. This kind of contemplation does not aim at making the mind inactive, but at quieting and unifying it in the midst of activity. Like Shakyamuni, afterwards we descend from the mountain into our place of work and responsibility.

In our congregational life, we can use the "choreography of the familiar" of Charles Moore. We know of maple trees, oak trees, apple trees, ash trees, but perhaps we might try to draw or make a Jesse tree. This is a special tree to remind us of the connection between the Hebrew Scriptures, or the Old Testament, and the New Testament—especially to be drawn during the Advent season. The type of tree we use is not important, either a small actual tree brought into a room or a tree which we draw, but the decorations we place on the tree or draw make the ordinary extraordinary. The tree is named after Jesse, the father of David, whom God appointed in the Hebrew Scriptures to serve as the king of Israel. David became the first member of a new royal family, ruling over Israel for many years; Matthew and Luke say in the New Testament that it was this royal family into which Jesus was born. These ancestors, in addition to all those who came later in the Hebrew Scriptures, make up the family and spiritual background of Jesus.

As we add our art forms to the Jesse tree, we are making Jesus' family tree. We draw or make one thing which will help us recall persons who have prepared the world for the coming of Christ. In Zen style, we simplify and concentrate on only one art symbol for each person despite the many-sided meaning of a Solomon, an Isaiah, a Mary. So, we might make or draw an ark for Noah, wedding raiment for Rebecca, a ladder for Jacob, a bright red bush for Moses, a heart for Ruth, a lily for Mary. As we move from the ordinariness of a tree to the extraordinariness of a symbol illuminating the Jewish background of Jesus, we might also think of our own families and our own symbols. What part of the Hebrew Scriptures might we choose to represent our families as they await the coming of Jesus or the coming of any event?

We might even place ourselves in visual art forms. To play a role in a Christmas or Easter pageant, entering into the familiarity and starkness of birth and death, to play the roles of Mary, Joseph, shepherds, magi in an outdoor nativity scene, standing or sitting for a period of time (wearing thermal underwear and shivering!)—all these are participative ways of allowing seeing to take place.

AESTHETICS AND COMPASSION

Tens of thousands of Americans have lost their lives to AIDS, to say nothing of the tremendous loss of lives in other areas, particularly Africa. An art venture related to AIDS was inaugurated in 1987 with the "Names Project Memorial Quilt." The giant quilt covering over one hundred thousand square feet is a national memorial to those Americans who have succumbed to AIDS. The quilt is made up of 3´ x 6´ fabric panels created by friends and families of those who have died.

Mothers, fathers, sisters, brothers, children, friends, lovers have joined in the making of the panels. The sections are spectacularly colorful and varied. The images are many: pets, seashells, suit jackets, Mardi Gras masks, rhinestones, cremation ashes, T-shirts, merit badges, first-place ribbons. The materials are sewn into the panels or drawn upon them. One panel is made from a Buddhist saffron robe, another from a solid 3´ x 6´ piece of leather.

95

Even those who had no connection with those who have died came to view the quilt and volunteer their help in laying out the panels. One such volunteer was quoted in the San Diego media: "I feel lucky that I don't know anyone to make a panel for. But even though I don't know anyone personally who died, these are my people, and I don't want these people to be forgotten. For the people who make the panels, it's like a final farewell, putting their friends to rest finally and getting on with things."

No other disease has called forth such an outpouring of artistic effort for those who suffer and for those who are close to them. Furthermore, the Names Project Memorial Quilt has, in a large part, brought other art projects into being. "Living through Art" is a theme for classes offering art therapy for people with life-threatening diseases. Perhaps through this use of the visual arts, hope may be given for the time remaining, and even dignity and purpose may be found in the threatening present. No particular skills are needed for this art therapy. People come with ideas of sharing and presenting—expressing their anger, sadness, and yet responsiveness.

The church should be a part of this national tragedy and concern and participate in the Names Project Memorial Quilt project. Familiar as it is with the meaning of death, crucifixion, and suffering, as well as with redemption, hope, and the presence of the Holy Spirit, the church might engage in its own visual art of quilt making, relating to this national epidemic. It might even inaugurate a quilting bee to form communities of people working together through art to call attention to the presence of the disease and the need for quickened research and progress toward a cure. Such a project would call attention to the needs of those with HIV/AIDS and their families and friends.

A church living aesthetically will find itself breaking new ground. There will be a cessation of old, desiccated ways and, perchance, an ecstatic movement toward freedom. Living aesthetically means responding to the sense of fullness and presence in beauty as well as to its absence and mystery—the fullness of Easter and the emptiness of Good Friday. Living aesthetically means a liberation in order to understand more fully the dimensions of life. Friedrich von Schiller, writing on aesthetics, said, "It is only through beauty that man makes his way to freedom."[3]

We must not ask too much of art. Even when it comes about as a "choreography of the familiar," even when we participate fully in its creation, even when we think we are seeing its meanings—even then, because of its own life and force, the significance will not be clear. Only scattered perceptions of presence and absence may be known to us in our aesthetic living, but we cling to these and nourish them. Martin Heidegger spoke of his philosophy as a "way," and he thought his philosophy was "on the way." So it is with our aesthetic experience—a way but not a conclusion.

William Ames (1576–1633), perhaps the foremost Puritan theologian, wrote at the very beginning of his *Medulla Theologiae*, or the *Marrow of Theology*, that theology is *"doctrina vivendi Deo*, or the teaching of living to God."[4] The visual arts offer us the chance to live to God in our comprehension and expression of what we understand to be the meaning of God in the world and in the living of our lives. Above all, art offers us in the church living aesthetically an experience of joy and responsiveness, often in a cheerless world.

Happiness:
Waking, alive again,
In this grey world of winter rain.
Shiba

FOR REFLECTION AND DISCUSSION

1. What do you see in your church's worship service that aids your faith—the altar, the cross, the windows (clear or stained glass), the procession/recession? Other?

2. A Zen Buddhist rock and stone garden, emphasizing emptiness, calm, simplicity, a feeling of home, could be a thing of beauty and spiritual resource to a sick, elder person. Could you make one for him or her? What might happen to you in the making?

3. How does the space of your favorite church sanctuary affect you? What do you see and feel in that space?

NOTES

INTRODUCTION: AESTHETICS IN RELIGION AND ART

1. Samuel Laeuchli, *Religion and Art in Conflict* (Philadelphia: Fortress Press, 1980).

2. Hans-Georg Gadamer, *Truth and Method* (London: Sheed and Ward, 1975), 63. See also Wassily Kandinsky, *On the Spiritual in Art* (New York: Solomon R. Guggenheim Foundation, 1946, and also several earlier editions).

3. Friedrich W. Nietzsche, *The Birth of Tragedy* in *Basic Writings of Nietzsche*, trans, ed. Walter Kaufmann (New York: Modern Library, 1968), 52.

4. Laurens van der Post, *Yet Being Someone Other* (New York: William Morrow, 1983), 234.

5. Martin Heidegger, *Poetry, Language, Thought* (New York: Harper and Row, 1975), 6.

1. AESTHETICS AND BEAUTY

1. See John D. Eusden, "Chartres and Ryoan-ji: Aesthetic Connections between Gothic Cathedral and Zen Garden," *Eastern Buddhist*, n.s. 18, no. 2 (autumn 1985). Re-published in *Cross Currents*, 1993.

2. Henry Adams, *Mont Saint-Michel and Chartres* (Boston: Houghton Mifflin, 1933), 377.

3. Clifford Geertz, *Local Knowledge: Further Essays in Interpretive Anthropology* (New York: Basic Books, 1983), 54, 47–48.

4. George Santayana, *The Sense of Beauty: Being the Outline of Aesthetic Theory* (New York: Dover Publications, 1955), 31ff.

5. Quoted in Geertz, *Local Knowledge*, 10.

6. Martin Heidegger, *Poetry, Language, Thought* (New York: Harper and Row, 1975), 5; Heidegger, *Basic Writings*, ed. David F. Krell (New York: Harper and Row, 1977), 91.

7. Quoted in *Harvard Library Bulletin*, 1954, 71.

8. Shigematsu Soiku, *A Zen Forest: Sayings of the Masters* (New York: Weatherhill, 1981), 111.

9. Ralph W. Emerson, "The American Scholar," in Stanley Cavell, *Pursuits of Happiness: The Hollywood Comedy of Remarriage* (Cambridge, Mass.: Harvard University Press, 1981), 14.

2. AESTHETICS AND TRUTH

1. Ho Tao, "The Landscape Painting of Huang Pin-hung: A Personal View," in *Innovation within Tradition: The Painting of Huang Pin-hung,* ed. Jason C. Kuo (Williamstown, Mass.: Williams College Museum of Art, 1989), 99.

2. Frederick Franck, *The Zen of Seeing* (New York: Random House, 1973), xi.

3. Douglas Bush, ed., *Selected Poems and Letters by John Keats* (Boston: Houghton Mifflin, 1959), 257.

3. AESTHETICS AND GOODNESS

1. Roland DeLattre, *Beauty and Sensibility in the Thought of Jonathan Edwards: An Essay in Aesthetics and Theological Ethics* (New Haven: Yale University Press, 1968), on which much of the above is based. Also, Robert W. Shahan and Kenneth R. Merrill, "Beauty and Politics: A Problematic Legacy of Jonathan Edwards," in *American Philosophy from Edwards to Quine* (Norman: University of Oklahoma Press, 1977).

2. Amos Wilder, *Grace Confounding Poems* (Philadelphia: Fortress, 1972), ix.

3. Iris Murdoch, *The Sovereignty of Good* (London: Routledge and Kegan Paul, 1970), 60.

4. Stanley Hauerwas, *Vision and Virtue* (Notre Dame, Ind.: Fides/Claretian, 1974), 39.

5. Much of the above is from Suzi Gablik, "Art beyond the Rectangle," *New Art Examiner,* December 1989.

4. HUMAN LIFE AND WHOLENESS

1. Iris Murdoch, *The Bell* (London: Chatto & Windus, 1958), 192.

2. Henry D. Thoreau, *Walden* (Princeton: Princeton University Press, 1989), 8.

3. Nishitani Keiji, *Religion and Nothingness* (Berkeley: University of California Press, 1982), 137.

4. Feng Gia-Fu and Jane English, eds., *Tao Te Ching* (New York: Random House, 1972), chap. 14.

5. WORSHIP AND PRAYER

1. Barry Lopez, "The Country of the Mind," in *Words from the Land: Encounters with Natural History Writing,* ed. Stephen Trimble (Salt Lake City: Gibbs Smith, 1989), 301–2.

6. LEARNING AND GROWTH

1. Oliver W. Sacks, *The Man Who Mistook His Wife for a Hat* (New York: Harper and Row, 1987).

2. Parker J. Palmer, *To Know As We Are Known* (San Francisco: Harper and Row, 1983), 25.

3. Madeleine L'Engle, *Walking on Water* (Wheaton, Ill.: Harold Shaw Publishers, 1980), 51.
4. Maria Harris, *Teaching and Religious Imagination* (San Francisco: Harper and Row, 1987), 155ff.

CONCLUSION: IMPLICATIONS OF AESTHETICS FOR THE CHURCH

1. John Dillenberger, "Visual Arts and Religion: Modern and Contemporary Contours," presidential address, *Journal of the American Academy of Religion* 56 (summer 1988): 199–212.
2. John W. Cook, *Arts: The Arts in Religious and Theological Studies* 1, no. 1 (June 1988).
3. Friedrich von Schiller, *On the Aesthetic Education of Man: In a Series of Letters,* ed. and trans. Elizabeth M. Wilkinson and L. A. Willoughby (Oxford: Clarendon Press, 1967), 9.
4. William Ames, *The Marrow of Theology,* trans., ed. John D. Eusden (Philadelphia: United Church Press, 1968, and Durham, N.C.: Labyrinth Press, 1983), 77.

SELECTED BIBLIOGRAPHY

Apostolos-Cappadona, Diane, ed. *Art, Creativity, and the Sacred*. New York: Crossroad, 1984.

Dewey, John. *Art as Experience*. New York: Perigee Books, 1934.

Dillenberger, John. *A Theology of Artistic Sensibilities*. New York: Crossroad, 1986.

Franck, Frederick. *The Zen of Seeing*. New York: Random House, 1973.

Gardner, Howard. *The Arts and Human Development*. New York: John Wiley and Sons, 1973.

Geertz, Clifford. *Local Knowledge: Further Essays in Interpretive Anthropology*. New York: Basic Books, 1983.

Harris, Maria. *Teaching and Religious Imagination*. San Francisco: Harper and Row, 1987.

Hauerwas, Stanley. *Vision and Virtue*. Notre Dame: Fides/Claretian, 1974.

Heidegger, Martin. *Poetry, Language, Thought*. New York: Harper and Row, 1975.

Jacobus, Lee. *Aesthetics and the Arts*. New York: McGraw-Hill, 1968.

Laeuchli, Samuel. *Religion and Art in Conflict*. Philadelphia: Fortress Press, 1980.

Kandinsky, Wassily. *On the Spiritual in Art*. New York: Solomon R. Guggenheim, 1946.

Louth, Andrew. *Discerning the Mystery*. New York: Clarendon Press, 1983.

Miles, Margaret. *Image as Insight*. Boston: Beacon Press, 1985.

Murdoch, Iris. *The Sovereignty of Good*. London: Routledge and Kegan Paul, 1970.

Nichols, Aiden. *The Art of God Incarnate*. New York: Paulist Press, 1980.

Read, Herbert. *The Meaning of Art*. Baltimore: Penguin Books, 1951.

Shigematsu Soiku. *A Zen Forest: Sayings of the Masters*. New York: Weatherhill, 1981.

Stewart, Harold, trans. *A Chime of Windbells: A Year of Japanese Haiku in English Verse*. Rutland, Vt.: Charles E. Tuttle, 1981.

Tillich, Paul. *On Art and Architecture*. New York: Crossroad, 1987.

Wilder, Amos. *Theopoetic*. Philadelphia: Fortress Press, 1976.

Wolterstorff, Nicholas. *Art in Action*. Grand Rapids, Mich.: Eerdmans, 1980.